Cambridge Elements

Elements in Travel Writing
edited by
Nandini Das
University of Oxford
Tim Youngs
Nottingham Trent University

WRITING ABOUT DISCOVERY IN THE EARLY MODERN EAST INDIES

Su Fang Ng
Virginia Polytechnic Institute and State University

Shaftesbury Road, Cambridge CB2 8EA, United Kingdom

One Liberty Plaza, 20th Floor, New York, NY 10006, USA

477 Williamstown Road, Port Melbourne, VIC 3207, Australia

314–321, 3rd Floor, Plot 3, Splendor Forum, Jasola District Centre,
New Delhi – 110025, India

103 Penang Road, #05–06/07, Visioncrest Commercial, Singapore 238467

Cambridge University Press is part of Cambridge University Press & Assessment,
a department of the University of Cambridge.

We share the University's mission to contribute to society through the pursuit of
education, learning and research at the highest international levels of excellence.

www.cambridge.org
Information on this title: www.cambridge.org/9781009045865

DOI: 10.1017/9781009047029

First published 2022

A catalogue record for this publication is available from the British Library.

ISBN 978-1-009-04586-5 Paperback
ISSN 2632-7090 (online)
ISSN 2632-7082 (print)

Writing about Discovery in the Early Modern East Indies

Elements in Travel Writing

DOI: 10.1017/9781009047029
First published online: November 2022

Su Fang Ng
Virginia Polytechnic Institute and State University

Author for correspondence: Su Fang Ng, ngsf@vt.edu

Abstract: Portuguese explorations opened the sea route to Asia, bringing armed trading to the Indian Ocean. This Element examines the impact of the 1511 Portuguese conquest of the port kingdom of Melaka on early travel literature. Putting into dialogue accounts from Portuguese, *mestiço*, and Malay perspectives, this study reexamines early modern "discovery" as a cross-cultural trope. Trade and travel were intertwined while structured by religion. Rather than newness or wonder, Portuguese representations focus on recovering what is known and grafting Asian knowledges – including local histories – onto European epistemologies. Framing Portuguese rule as a continuation of the sultanate, they re-spatialize Melaka into a European city. However, this model is complicated by a second one of accidental discovery facilitated by native agents. For Malay texts too, travel traverses known routes and spaces. Malay travelers insert themselves into foreign spaces by forging new kinship alliances, even as indigenous networks are increasingly disrupted by European incursions.

Keywords: Melaka, Southeast Asia, Tomé Pires, Manuel Godinho de Erédia, Hang Tuah

ISBNs: 9781009045865 (PB), 9781009047029 (OC)
ISSNs: 2632-7090 (online), 2632-7082 (print)

Contents

1 Introduction: Indian Ocean Travel Networks in Early Modernity

Discussing cannabis in the Eighth Colloquy of his *Colloquies on the Simples and Drugs of India* (*Colóquios dos simples e drogas da India*, Goa, 1563), a Portuguese physician in Goa, Garcia da Orta (1501–68), offers a story that purports to reveal native attitudes on travel: "The great Sultan Bahadur said to Martim Afonso de Sousa, to whom he wished every good thing and to whom he told his secrets, that when, at night, he wanted to go to Portugal, Brazil, Turkey, Arabia, or Persia, he only had to take a little BANGUE" (Orta, *Colloquies* 55).[1] The sultan substitutes actual travel, with all its deprivations, discomforts, and hardships, with an imaginary journey induced by psychedelic drugs. The resulting sensory experience retains only the pleasures and none of the pain of travel. His interlocutor, Martim Afonso de Sousa, on the other hand, commanded the first Portuguese expedition to Brazil and became its first royal governor. Thus, armchair travel is set against real-world explorations. The story also seems to invert the travel experience of Orta himself, whose important work on Asian *materia medica*, with wide circulation in Europe in translation, was the result of a long residence in Goa of almost thirty years, and who, like de Sousa, had natives tell him secrets, though in this case the secrets of nature.[2]

Yet Orta's image of Eastern indolence, even dissipated languor, is belied by the rather different portrait of Sultan Bahadur Shah of Gujarat (d. 1537) in a Ḥaḍramī chronicle, *Tārikh al-Shihrī* (*Annals of Shihr*, 1536–37 CE/943 H), also known as *Tārikh al-Ḥaḍramawt*. Cutting an active military figure there, the sultan is depicted as having a keen interest in travel:

> [T]hey [the Portuguese] reproached him [Sultan Bahadur] for sending ... the sailing-ships to Jeddah as already mentioned, (maintaining) that all he (really) intended was to incite the Turks (Arwām) against them. He (for his part) absolved himself, saying: "My intention was merely to go on the pilgrimage in them, but nobody apart from the minister (*al-wazīr*) and some of my family (*ahl-nā*) consented to go on the pilgrimage." They would not, however, believe him, and when he left them they sent two grabs in pursuit of him, but he fought them bravely till he and the ministers accompanying him were slain, all except the Khawādjā Safar, for him they spared. (Serjeant, *Portuguese* 75–76)[3]

[1] Although Markham identifies this as opium, which comes from the poppy plant, Indian *bhang* (from the Sanskrit *bhanga*, meaning "broken") is prepared from marijuana; his translation, with spelling silently corrected.

[2] On Orta and the hybridization of medicine see Cook, *Matters of Exchange* 96–99, 197–200, and essays in Costa, *Medicine, Trade and Empire*.

[3] Due to warfare with the Mughals, Bahadur was forced into an alliance with the Portuguese. Misunderstandings led to this outbreak of conflict.

In *Tārikh al-Shihrī*, it is the Portuguese who object to the sultan's investment in long-distance voyaging. Bahadur himself avers his "intention ... to go on pilgrimage," even if his will to travel was enacted by agents and representatives.

Despite Orta's image of Sultan Bahadur as a homebody holding travel at arm's length, ironically, conflict with the Portuguese over control of travel routes led to Sultan Bahadur's death. Portuguese suspicions might have had merit. Having lost a large part of his territory to the Mughals, Bahadur turned to the Portuguese for help – Martim Afonso de Souza was among those fighting the Mughals with Bahadur's forces in 1535 – but, regretting letting them build a fort at Diu, he tried to get them to return to Goa.[4] Even after news of Bahadur's death (the incident just described), his minister and envoy to Jeddah, Asaf Khan, persuaded the Ottomans to send a fleet to India. While their sailing was delayed, in 1538, the Ottomans, led by Hadim Süleiman Pasha, aided Gujarati forces, albeit unsuccessfully, to besiege Portuguese-occupied Diu.

The maritime route between Jeddah and Gujarat, then known to Europeans as Cambay, its primary port city, was part of a network connecting the Middle East to India and beyond. The network stretches far to the east to the Maluku Islands, the source of nutmeg and cloves, in the Indonesian Archipelago, which had as its primary entrepôt the city of Melaka, noted even by the earliest Portuguese commentators. Portuguese intervention tried to break those ties to transfer Indian Ocean networks into their control. Following a series of early conquests of key ports from India to Southeast Asia – Cochin (1504), Goa (1510), Melaka (1511), and Hormuz (1515) – they built forts and instituted a system of letters of marque to control shipping. The locations of the sultan's night journey in Orta's anecdote are not random. His dream circuit notably combines Indo-Persian spaces with those of the Portuguese colonial empire.

These juxtaposed stories suggest what is at stake in early modern travel and its narrations. First, Orta's anecdote raises the question of how foreign spaces are known. The Portuguese emphasize travel as experiential knowledge production. Sousa not only "discovers" Brazil; his travel to Gujarat gains him Bahadur's "secrets." Second, if travel promotes knowledge, travel curiosity has complex motivations. Early modern travel was driven by entangled political, economic, and religious aims. While economics drove political alliances, there were nonetheless religious considerations even if alliances were made and broken across faiths. If the Portuguese sought converts in Asia, Indian Ocean

[4] For the negotiations, see Flores, *Unwanted Neighbours*; on the voyage to Jeddah, see Alam and Subrahmanyam, "View from Mecca." Orta was present at the signing of the treaty between Nuno de Cunha and Bahadur on December 23, 1534. On the Portuguese empire in Asia see Subrahmanyam, *Portuguese Empire*; Pearson, *Portuguese in India*; and Flores, *Unwanted Neighbours*.

Muslims had as a model of travel the religious pilgrimage, the Hajj, to Mecca. Third, these narratives reveal the Indian Ocean's preexisting maritime network as well as Portuguese encroachment in that network. Portuguese travel writing plays a crucial role in securing these routes, delineating them to make trade routes visible for conquest and management. Fourth, in the early modern period, European and non-European circuits of travel also started to dovetail. Rather than creating or "discovering" new routes in the Indian Ocean, Europeans traversed established routes and even replicated preexisting port cities, sometimes in the same location. Thus, as they traveled the same circuits, Europeans and Asians started having common experiences of travel and wrote about them.

I examine early travel writings about one such port city, Melaka, which the Portuguese captured in 1511, their second major conquest after Goa. The explosion of European travel writing on Asia commenced with the start of Iberian long-distance voyaging at the end of the fifteenth century. In the European search for spices, Southeast Asia was particularly important. Cloves, mace, and nutmeg were found only in the Maluku Islands, known as the Spice Islands, in eastern Indonesia. Portuguese success in breaking the Arab-Venetian monopoly over the overland spice route spurred other Europeans to fund their own voyages of exploration, and the Maluku Islands were the focus of Portugal's territorial dispute with Spain such that after the 1494 Treaty of Tordesillas divided the New World, the 1529 Treaty of Zaragoza was signed to establish a Pacific meridian line. The distribution center for this commerce was Melaka, the region's preeminent entrepôt before Portuguese arrival. Its capture was a major victory that King Manuel I (r. 1495–1521) celebrated with an embassy to Pope Leo X in 1514, accompanied by exotic gifts, including the famed elephant Hanno.

Melaka's importance was not just regional. If the Gujarat-Jeddah line constituted one major arm of the Indian Ocean system, the other reached out to the Malay Archipelago. Shipping to the Red Sea came also from Southeast Asia: *Tārikh al-Shihrī* notes the expected arrival of the "Jeddah trade-fleet (*mūsim*), coming from the island of Atcheh [Aceh]" (Serjeant, *Portuguese* 110). Connected to the west to Gujarat, and thence to Red Sea ports like Jeddah, and to the east to China, Melaka lay at the crossroads of global maritime trade routes.

Portuguese writings about Melaka were the earliest European accounts of the city and the region.[5] Portuguese travel writing set the template for ethnographic description of other cultures. Ângela Barreto Xavier and Ines G. Županov argue

[5] While Marco Polo sailed the Strait of Melaka, he made no mention of Melaka. Ibn Battuta stayed three days in 1345 in a place he calls "Mul Jawa" (مل جاوة), sometimes identified as Melaka though its foundation date is under dispute (Ibn Battuta, *Voyages* 4: 239).

that the structure of early chronicles of expansion, such as those by João de Barros and Fernão Lopes de Castanheda, whereby "[t]he descriptions of the local customs were placed frequently in specific chapters, concerning geographical, political, and cultural aspects ... became a blueprint for other texts" (Xavier and Županov, *Catholic Orientalism* 21). Such organization is evident in the works I consider here, Tomé Pires's *Suma oriental* and Manuel Godinho de Erédia's descriptions of the region. In contrast, Malay writing about Melaka took the form of the chronicle history of the Malay sultanate, *Sulalat us-salatin* (*Genealogy of Kings*), otherwise known as *Sejarah Melayu* (*Malay Annals*), which inspired the prose romance *Hikayat Hang Tuah* (*The Story of Hang Tuah*, ca. 1680s), the subject of Section 4. While not conforming generically to European travel writing, their embedded travel narratives describe relations between the self and the world. Importantly, they challenge the narrative of the traveler as Western and travel literature as a European genre.

Scholarship on travel literature tends to focus on European works, whether the great early modern compilations, or, in Southeast Asia, colonial-period works by European administrators, officials, and adventurers, along with the occasional white raja. One departure from this scholarly neglect is Muzaffar Alam and Sanjay Subrahmanyam's *Indo-Persian Travels in the Age of Discoveries 1400–1800*. But even they, noting the "uneven distribution of travel-literature" in Asia, with a "curiously barren South Asian vernacular landscape" versus "the very richest of ... corpuses ... in Chinese," judge the poverty of travel accounts in South Asia vernaculars to be "[r]ather like a neighbouring literature, that in Malay" (Alam and Subrahmanyam, *Indo-Persian* 11–12). Malay travel writing's putative beginnings in the nineteenth century, defined by texts written by native interpreters to British colonial officers and traders, has led to the view that it emerged out of the encounter with European modernity. A Malay *munshi*, or language teacher, Ahmad Rijaluddin, traveled with Penang trader Robert Scott on one of the latter's visits to Calcutta in 1810 to advise Governor-General Lord Minto on the impending invasion of Java. Rijaluddin's account of Bengal is characterized as "a travel-diary, a form ... first met with during, and is probably symptomatic of, a transitional stage between a 'classical' and a 'modern' literature," arisen out of "the 'shock' of contact with the European colonial powers" (Skinner, "Transitional Malay Literature" 467–68). In attributing to it a European character, the implicit assumption is that Malay travelogues are Western imitations.

Traditions of travel writing exist in Arabic and Persian and influenced Malay. The conventions of the medieval Arabic genre of *riḥla*, narratives of travel, were established by the geographer Ahmad ibn Jubayr (1145–1217) in an influential account, *Riḥla*, of his 1183–84 pilgrimage from Granada to

Mecca.[6] The Muslim Hajj was also important to Southeast Asia and one early account is embedded in a "classical" text (Hooker and Milner, *Perceptions*).[7] Indeed, Ahmad Rijaluddin's father, Hakim Long Fakir Kandu, a prominent Chulia merchant and patriarch of a family of colonial scribes, owned a manuscript of this text, *Hikayat Hang Tuah*.[8] Representations of India by travelers from Southeast Asia include an embedded account of a voyage to Bengal in Ridjali's history of Amboyna, *Hikayat Hitu* (ca. 1650) (B. Andaya, "Imagination"). While the first-person narrative was still to come, already in classical Malay literature narratives of journeys rendered a picture of the wider world.

For even European travel writing has eluded strict definition to include a plethora of genres – prose and poetry, fact and fiction – to seem almost synonymous with writing itself: "Every story is a travel story" (Certeau, *Practice of Everyday Life* 115). While modern travel writing coalesces around the individual traveler and his or her experience, such a framework does not serve premodern texts well. Even for European works, Jorge Flores comments on the "strong tendency to see each author as a traveller who had his own agenda and to see each text as a milestone in travel literature" that has excluded authors like Erédia, discussed in Section 3, who fell outside of the "main collections of travel writing" (Flores, "Two Portuguese Visions" 47). More useful is Joan-Pau Rubiés's definition of works of literature that instead "share travel as their essential condition of production" (Rubiés, "Travel Writing" 6). This broader definition better accounts for bureaucratic reports and ship logs, merchant accounts, and poetic and prose epics and romances such as Luís Vaz de Camões's *Os Lusíadas* (1572) or its Malay analogue, *Hikayat Hang Tuah*.

The bulk of early modern European travel accounts of the East Indies was driven by commerce, though religious proselytization constituted a significant subsidiary motive. Trade was equally important to indigenous travel, and religious pilgrimage from Islamicate Southeast Asia was closely linked to commerce. Indeed, just as pilgrimage was one of the major reasons for travel in the Christian world, the Hajj, one of the Five Pillars of Islam, was and remains central in structuring travel for the Muslim world, as Bahadur's case shows. Eric Tagliocozzo finds in the seventeenth century a spike of Malay texts, including *Hikayat Hang Tuah*, that reference the Hajj, comment on religious Hajjis' movements around the Indian Ocean, and "mention … the Prophet's

[6] Netton, "Riḥla," 328; Touati, *Islam and Travel* 2, 11–12, 246–50; Beckingham, "The Riḥla."

[7] On the Hajj from Southeast Asia, see Roff, "Islamic Institutions" and "Pilgrimage"; Tagliacozzo, *Longest Journey*.

[8] This manuscript is at the British Library: Add MS 12384. See Skinner's translation and Nasution, *Chulia*.

Arabian cities and the pilgrimage, generally, as part of the fabric of their texts" (Tagliocozzo, *Longest Journey* 87). Both Portuguese and Malay travel writing, conceived broadly, exhibit the entanglement of trade and religion in the journeys they narrate.

To rephrase Rubiés's definition, movement is central to travel writing. For Michel de Certeau, a travel story is a "spatial practice": while "place (*lieu*) is the order," implying "stability," space [*espace*] is unstable, "composed of intersections of mobile elements . . . Space occurs as the effect produced by the operations that orient it, situate it, temporalize it, and make it function in a polyvalent unity of conflictual programs or contractual proximities . . . *space is a practiced place*" (Certeau, *Practice of Everyday Life* 117). To travel is to move away from home and toward the other. Any spatial practice inevitably comes up against other, contrary, practices. The works I read re-spatialize what had come before: for the Portuguese, the previous order defined by the Malay sultanate, and, for the Malay *Hikayat Hang Tuah*, opening up the global space to insert themselves in it while forced to grapple with Portuguese presence.

Spatial practices evoke affect in readers. In early narratives of Melaka, the primary affect is not wonder despite its apparent centrality, as Jonathan Sell asserts: "With respect to travel literature, the appropriate *ethos* was wonder. Not only does the encounter with the new provoke wonderment, but travel literature in the period that concerns us still had the blood of medieval *mirabilia* running through its veins" (Sell, *Rhetoric and Wonder* 57). This was not always the case. Consider Bahadur. Painted as apathetic, he represented himself (through Orta's account) as simply doing something mundane, practicing a religious duty. The travel texts I examine describe centuries-old trade routes; the evocation is rather of quite ordinary feelings.

Knowledge-making through writing travel is not necessarily the discovery of newness evoking wonder. Michael Pearson has observed how Portuguese chroniclers "desire to find familiar things in Asia," looking for similarities rather than differences (Pearson, *Portuguese in India* 116). This interpretive mode turns discovery into matters prosaic. As James Fleming points out, early moderns did not make a sharp distinction between invention and discovery, between "making and finding" (Fleming, *Invention* 2). Discovery was closely tied to recovery, as for instance, the Greco-Roman classics, and thus was a search for the expected. The idea of discovery as happening upon the unexpected was a different but coexisting model. Arguing for discovery's invention in a hermeneutics that "co-ordinates a proper scientific relationship" from the accidents of facts, Fleming identifies "a correlate of surprise" (185).

Surprise relates less to the first and more to the second even as scientific theory domesticates wonderment into comprehensibility. The first model is best articulated in William Eamon's well-known work on the hunt, or Latin *venatio*, as a metaphor for scientific discovery: "Just as the hunter tracks his hidden prey following its spoor, the hunter of secrets looks for traces, signs, and clues that will lead to the discovery of nature's hidden causes" (Eamon, *Science* 269). But, as Piers Brown notes, this method implies foreknowledge. Discussing Johannes Kepler's use of the travel narrative metaphor, Brown elaborates on Fleming's accidental surprise, arguing for a "hermeneutics of discovery that focuses on error as beneficial precisely because of the accidental discoveries it produces" (Brown, "Travel Narratives" 17).

For the travel writers I read, the model of finding the expected or making what is found conform to what is already known still largely prevails, though we start to see a tension between the two. Still useful is Vitorino Magalhães Godinho's articulation of the early modern Portuguese definition of "discovery" (*descobrimento*). More than just an uncovering of the unknown, it has a precise definition: "To apprehend space and spaces is to go in search of what is suspected to exist but is unknown . . . But the real key of discovery is to be able to trace a route for going back to the originating port; and later to know how to go again to where one was, and to return safely" (*Apreender o espaço e os espaços, é ir em busca ou do que se suspeita existir mas se desconhece . . . Mas a verdadeira chave do descobrir é conseguir traçar a rota para regressar ao porto de largada; e depois saber tornar a ir onde se foi, e regressar de novo a salvo*) (Godinho, "Ideia de descobrimento" 633, my translation).

Rather than finding out the absolutely new for the first time – rather than priority or originality – it is a recovery. Josiah Blackmore further notes that the concept of the way (*caminho*) in Portuguese nautical narratives is not orientation free but "usually implies a general movement in a certain and predetermined direction" (Blackmore, *Moorings* 59). Godinho's definition is performed in iterations, for the "embedded traveler/writer" moving through space "enacts a repetitiveness of encounter with the natural and human worlds that establishes *saber* or knowledge" (61). This recovery is transnational and, I suggest, transactional. "Discovery" or *descobrimento* is an epistemological ascertaining and confirmation of a preexisting Asian network of trade routes. While the Portuguese emphasized travel as experiential knowledge production, that knowledge was understood as already known. However, one of the authors I read is fascinated with discovery arising from haphazard and unexpected accidents. In the work of Erédia, the widening fissure between the two models is most evident.

Existing knowledge is not just European but also non-European. Portuguese travel writing serves the purpose of acquiring and translating indigenous knowledges to be grafted onto European epistemologies.[9] The two Portuguese authors I discuss re-spatialize Melaka in part by turning to native knowledges and indigenous chronicles. To a greater or lesser extent, all three authors and/or texts considered here engage with some version of indigenous history of Melaka that would become *Sejarah Melayu* (*Malay Annals*). Section 2 focuses on Tomé Pires's *Suma oriental*, which, in giving an itinerary from the Red Sea to the East Indies, frames Melaka not as a place of marvels but as a destination. The general affect is thus of ordinary mundaneness to make Melaka a suitable settlement. Pires has a settler colonialist's pragmatism. Section 3 considers the writings of *mestiço* Manuel Godinho de Erédia, who also turns to native sources. However, he displays a tension between the prevalent idea of discovery as recovering what is known and the alternate model of questing for the new. While fitting Southeast Asia into ancient and biblical frameworks, especially Solomon's relations with Ophir, he repeatedly turns to the idea of accidental discovery, usually a shipwreck, revealing new lands. I argue that these accidental discoveries often rely on native agents.

For Malay texts too, travel traverses known routes and spaces. The issue is how to insert oneself into a known, but foreign, space. Section 4 examines *Hikayat Hang Tuah*, a fictionalizing of *Sejarah Melayu*. Its protagonist embarks on commerce-driven ambassadorial journeys through the Indian Ocean along well-traveled routes. Trade relations are forged through kinship alliances, including marriage diplomacy. The text also re-spatializes the Indian Ocean; but rather than remaking the landscape, it diplomatically inserts Malays into an established network of centers of political and religious power. Hang Tuah engages in such modes of integration as rituals of adoption. However, this mode of travel is increasingly disrupted by Portuguese bellicosity.

This Element puts into dialogue early Portuguese and Malay travel narratives to reexamine the rhetoric of discovery as a cross-cultural trope and the connected histories of travel writing as a genre. These three figures – Pires, Erédia, and Hang Tuah – represent a new efflorescence of early modern travel writing that crossed cultural boundaries. Furthermore, trade and travel are intertwined even as travel is also structured by religion and the texts are influenced by genres of religious writing. Pires's *Suma oriental* is organized like a pilgrim's manual or guide. Erédia turns to the biblical story of Ophir's missions to King Solomon to locate Southeast Asia. *Hikayat Hang Tuah* weaves into its secular

[9] *Translatio* also means "to graft": *translatio* "first appeared in the sense of 'change,' even of address, 'transport,' banking operation, botanical graft, and metaphor" (Eco, *Experiences* 74). Orta was an adept engrafter of Indian botanical knowledge.

travel account, *riḥla sifariyya*, a religious Hajj, the pilgrimage to Mecca enjoined by Islam.

Travel was not simply an individual affair. Just as pilgrimages had fixed itineraries, premodern secular travel had stable transnational circuits with set centers and nodes within those circuits. If travel writing is knowledge-making, it seeks out information beyond its linguistic or ethnic communities. This incorporation of foreign knowledge and its circulation link together East and West. Even when travel is troped as "discovery," shared destinations – both religious and secular – and shared knowledges shape early modern itineraries and make such journeys communal enterprises. We find the entanglement of Malay and Portuguese knowledges in the beginnings of travel literature of *India Meridionale*, the southern Indies, as Erédia calls Southeast Asia, as they strive to describe and to comprehend Melaka as a city of international trade.

2 Tomé Pires and the Way to Melaka

> "[Melaka] is at the end of the monsoons, where you find what you want, and sometimes more than you are looking for."[10]

Tomé Pires (1465–1524 or 1540) was one of the first European authors to give a detailed description of Melaka and Southeast Asia. His eyewitness account, *Suma oriental* (ca. 1512–15), was one of the best-informed early works. While early Iberian travel literature heavily emphasizes discovery and conquest – in Portugal, starting with Zurara's fifteenth-century *Chronicle of the Discovery and Conquest of Guinea* – Pires's narrative differed from the chroniclers in focusing not on Portuguese deeds but rather on the peoples and lands of Asia. Ângela Barreto Xavier and Ines Županov contend, "geography was the main protagonist of Pires's book" (Xavier and Županov, *Catholic Orientalism* 120). Pires's work is most comparable to that of Duarte Barbosa (d. 1545), whose employment in the Kochi factory and knowledge of Malayalam allowed him to write a detailed ethnography of India and other places around the Indian Ocean in his *Livro* (ca. 1516).[11]

Pires too was locally informed. A factor of "drugs" (spices), an apothecary by training, who supervised the spice trade in Melaka from 1512 to 1515, he was thoroughly familiar with the region. His knowledge of Southeast Asia was superior to that of Barbosa or Orta, both based in India. Pires's *Suma* remained

[10] Pires, *Suma oriental*, 228. Citations are from the English translation of Cortesão's 1944 edition in two volumes but with continuous pagination. Citations are given parenthetically; when citing the Portuguese original I reference Loureiro's edition of the Paris manuscript by editor's name; occasionally I revise the translation silently for clarity.

[11] For an English version, see Dames's translation of Barbosa. On his ethnography in the context of European travel to India, see Rubiés, *Travel* 99, 220–22.

in manuscript, though it circulated in Goa, and was not published in its entirety until its discovery in Paris in 1944.[12] By the mid-sixteenth century, information about Portuguese India became more widely known and a portion of Pires's *Suma oriental* was translated and published in the first volume, *Primo*, of Giovanni Battista Ramusio's great compilation, *Navigationi et viaggi* (1550), the pioneering compendium that would be the first of increasing numbers of large collections of travel literature.

The work's title, *Suma oriental*, hints at how Pires viewed it – as akin to the medieval genre of the *summa*, a comprehensive summation that systematically organizes and synthesizes knowledge of Asia.[13] While Pires's work, like a *summa*, aims at a synthetic view from a single, unitary perspective – and thus has an authorial point of view – unlike modern travel writing or even some early modern travelogues, it does not present the author as a heroic traveler-writer. Yet it is undoubtedly a work that arose from Pires's travel to the Indies. As Kim Phillips notes, information from physical travel is transformed through iterative reproduction into "related literary form, such as a geography, encyclopaedia, *summa* or romance" (Phillips, "Travel, Writing" 82). But if modeled after a medieval scholastic genre, Pires's *Suma* is remarkably free of medieval myths about the foreign or the Torrid Zone. Mention of men with big ears, reminiscent of Pliny, is brought up only to be immediately dismissed. This despite its place in the first explosion of travel literature from European expansionism, which extensively retailed marvels: regarding Hispanic writing on the New World, Neil Whitehead finds that the sheer volume of works "filled with the discovery of the fantastic, the survival of the anachronistic, and the promise of marvelous monstrosity" made the exotic ordinary (Whitehead, "South America/Amazonia" 122).

In the relative absence of exoticization, *Suma oriental* offers instead practical information. Take, for instance, Pires's treatment of the durian fruit native to Southeast Asia. Even today its pungent smell is widely known to send Europeans reeling: in the nineteenth century, William Marsden describes it as a "rich fruit, but strong, and even offensive, in taste as well as smell" (Marsden, *History of Sumatra* 98). Pires, however, considers it "lovelier and more delicious than all the other fruits" (137) and "the best fruit in the world" (260), the latter judgment forming part of a note on fruit farms around Melaka. Instead of turning the unfamiliar fruit into an object of marvel, Pires normalizes it by

[12] The *sigilo* school attributes this to the Portuguese crown's tight control over information on Indies explorations, especially the Spice Islands. For its circulation in Goa, see Xavier and Županov, *Catholic Orientalism* 88.

[13] The *summa* differs from the encyclopedia as "almost always an authored text [that] tends towards synthesis and a degree of ideological unity" (Franklin-Brown, *Reading the World* 69).

underlining its commercial value. His high praise suggests the adoption of a local perspective. The fruit farms, called *dusun* in Malay, would become the subject of contention in the next decade between Portuguese *casados*, or settled householders, and the Tamil South Indian merchant community of Melaka (Subrahmanyam, "What the Tamils Said" 147–50). I read Pires not in terms of the familiar narrative of a teleological progression to a rational early modernity. Scholars observe the continuity from the medieval to the early modern periods in beliefs in the supernatural; among them, Jorge Flores shows how stories of marvels circulated between South Asia and Portugal and the rest of Europe. Rather, in eschewing exoticism, Pires's presentation of Asia focuses strongly on trade and its commercial potential. His rhetorical purpose is to encourage settler colonialism. He depicts Southeast Asia as comprising highly connected trading networks. A social historiographer, Pires is concerned with various trading alliances and rivalries, information useful for settlement.

Rather than an account of personal experience, Pires's *Suma oriental* is an itinerary. Organized as a kind of narrative rutter, the chapters describe places and peoples along the route from the Red Sea to the Malay Archipelago. The book's structure allows the reader to spatialize the Indian Ocean; it is a "route tour," not unlike Spanish cartographic literature that "brings the narratee into the space being described" (Padrón, "Hybrid Maps" 206). Ricardo Padrón even compares portolan charts to the "unidimensionality of the discursive itinerary" (Padrón, *Spacious Word* 62). Resembling the pragmatic navigational rutter (*roteiro* in Portuguese), *Suma oriental*'s structure also suggests the influence of medieval pilgrimage manuals (*itineraria*) with commentary on the people and route along the way but, importantly, a set destination as the journey's culmination. (Pilgrimage guides existed for both Christians and Muslims.) If *Suma oriental* is a text of secular pilgrimage, then Melaka is its Jerusalem. Pires devotes an entire unit to Melaka, placing it at the climactic end of the work; he privileges Melaka even over the famed Spice Islands. While using the medieval rhetoric of the "edge of the world," Pires reverses the medieval mode of talking about near and far places. Marco Polo and Mandeville exaggerate the exoticism of far places but Pires gives Melaka "at the end of the monsoons" the most detailed description with a substantial history. The concluding sixth book examines in detail Melaka's history, geography, and political administration. Pires's deep interest in the social landscape, motivated by trade, leads him to incorporate local history substantially into his narrative. Although attention to Melaka's foundation suggests the use of native sources, the text also, I argue, frames Portuguese rule as a continuation of the previous kingdom. Both the pragmatism and the incorporation of the Portuguese as successors come from a settler perspective. For that reason, Pires positions Melaka as part of the known world. But first I consider his description of the Indian Ocean world as context.

2.1 Trade and Religion

Pires, in his dedicatory preface, articulates the same two goals Vasco da Gama purportedly expressed upon his arrival in Calicut (Kerala): "We come in search of Christians and spices" (Gama, *Em nome de Deus* 71). Praising Manuel I's large armada, Pires extols the extension of Portuguese imperial power through warfare conducted by Afonso de Albuquerque, who "never ceases fighting against the name of Mohammed" (2; Loureiro 50). Simultaneously, he announces his subject to be "trading in merchandise . . . that ennobles kingdoms and makes their people great" (4). The twin objectives of trade and religion shape his account of the Indies. *Suma oriental* is less a geography than a peoplescape, an ethnography concerned with the inhabitants' religion, openness to trade, and race.

While *Suma oriental* is ostensibly organized into geographical regions whose boundaries are defined by the major Asian rivers – the Nile, Tigris, Euphrates, Indus, and Ganges – its dominant attention to trade and to trading partners (or warring enemies) means it is an itinerary structured by destinations. Melaka is the culminating terminus but along the route lie a number of way stations. In describing countries, Pires pays particular attention to chief cities and major ports. He delineates Cairo's political system but, with ports such as Aden, he homes in on their defensive fortresses and delves into their trade.

Details on trade include lists not simply of products but also of trading partners. Products are linked to specific partners, whether goods were sent or received. Some of the linkages involve more than one place – for instance, Aden takes merchandise procured from Cairo to Ormuz and to Cambay (Gujarat). From Cambay Aden gets cloth, which is traded to Arabia and the Islands. Melaka, though at the end of Pires's itinerary, is an important trading partner for Aden at the other end of the Indian Ocean. Merchandise from Melaka, "chiefly spices and drugs," are taken to Bengal and to Pegu in exchange for other goods (16). Cairo is particularly important for Aden, and Pires includes information on alternative routes there, giving the journey's duration, the security of the route, and the stops along the way.

Pires is thus describing a network. Ports are distribution hubs with goods and merchants coming and going. But while Aden is one of the largest hubs, this pattern of the flow of goods is replicated throughout the Indian Ocean with different ports driving greater or lesser trade. One significant hub was Cambay, described as "stretch[ing] out two arms . . . towards Aden and . . . towards Malacca, as the most important places to sail to" (42). In a network, ports are interdependent: "Malacca cannot live without Cambay, nor Cambay without Malacca" (45).

Cambay, the major port of Gujarat, retained its importance a hundred years later when the next author I discuss, Manuel Godinho de Erédia, identified it as the kingdom of the greatest antiquity in Hindustan (Hosten, "Description" 542). Christopher Wake notes that in Pires one "can discern the general outlines of a pattern of trading relations which linked the various ports of Java and Melaka" before the changes caused by the Portuguese presence (Wake, "Banten" 70). Viewed as a whole, the most important commercial center of this network, Melaka, is located at its edges. For many of the ports he describes, Pires deliberately includes their relation to Melaka, the primary geographical reference point. All roads lead to Melaka. The network thus retains the linearity of an itinerary. It matters where one ends up.

Trade involves not just goods but people. Traders are travelers. Some are particularly mobile: the natives of Kalinga "scattered from here all over the three Indias" (65), such that Pires discusses them in several separate places. A kingdom's ability to attract foreign merchants is a measure of its power. A port's importance is gauged by how cosmopolitan it is. Pires admiringly notes that "very often eighty-four languages have been found spoken . . . in Malacca alone" (2:269). His description reverses the direction of trade, focusing on what is imported rather than on what is exported in order to emphasize Melaka's status as an entrepôt. Such a cosmopolitan port constitutes an administrative challenge, which Pires describes in Book 6.

Melaka's attraction for foreign traders is the commercial corollary to the measure by which Indian Ocean monarchs gauge their power. Stanley Tambiah has argued that states from Sri Lanka to the Indonesian Archipelago were galactic states with political authority radiating out from sacral centers with weakening spheres of control (Tambiah, "Galactic Polity"). Native kings in Southeast Asia welcomed Europeans because they added to their power, and sometimes Europeans were seen as potential new allies against local rivals.

Pires's ethnography has a strong commercial bent. As a social ethnographer, Pires attends most to three characteristics as he traverses the Indian Ocean: religion, propensity for trade, and skin color. The first is a continuation of the Iberian late medieval war against Muslims. This strand in *Suma oriental* replicates the chivalric values of the crusading era. While Pires does not explicitly seek out the legendary Prester John, the Christian king in the East, he searches for and identifies Christians wherever he finds them. The second, propensity for trade, can be seen as an extension of the idea of a continuum of humanity inherited from Greco-Roman notions about civility. If, for the Greeks and Romans, the eloquent use of persuasive speech distinguishes the civilized from the barbarians, for Pires, civilizational potential is marked by propensity for trade. Trading is fundamentally a form of communication.

To start with, Pires sees Portuguese expansion as part of a holy war against Islam, importing earlier ideas of crusade into Asia. Yet, because Muslims dominated the Indian Ocean, the Portuguese were forced to cooperate with them. At the same time awareness was growing of other religions in Asia. Lumping non-Muslims and non-Christians into the category of heathens, Pires views them as potential converts, especially those, such as the Moluccans, who have not been Muslims long. Pires asserts that they "sigh for us" ("*sospirã por nos*," 207; Loureiro 223). He also makes much of intra-Muslim conflict, dwelling, for instance, on the Sunni-Shia schism in his discussion of Persia (24–26).

More so than Muslims, Christians fascinate Pires, recalling the European search for Prester John. Vasco da Gama's 1497 expedition even carried a letter from King Manuel to Prester John (Gama, *Em nome de Deus* 23, 30). Pires's survey reveals the diversity of Christians in Asia, from Abyssinians to Malabars, converted by St. Thomas. In taking an expansive approach to look for allies, he can be too quick to detect covert, former, or potential Christians. He repeats the rumor that the prophet Muhammad's four followers were Christians, emphasizes Persia's Sheikh Ismail's upbringing by Christian relations, and mentions Christian renegades employed by Muslim princes.

Pires uncovers Christians where they don't exist, including the Hindu Banians of Cambay (Gujarat), who "believe in Our Lady and in the Trinity" (39). This misinterpretation of the Hindu threefold god was current among the Portuguese of the time: "The whole of Malabar believes, as we do, in the Trinity of Father, Son and Holy Ghost, three in one, the only true God. From Cambay to Bengal all the people hold this [faith]" (66), but they are full of "very heathen practices" (72). As Michael Pearson notes, Portuguese travelers and chroniclers looked for similarities rather than differences, especially in religious practices (Pearson, *Portuguese in India* 116).

More than simply a habit of mind, Pires's search for Christians stems from a Manueline imperial vision. Building on Jean Aubin's work on Portuguese diplomacy with Ethiopia arising from the search for Prester John, Luís Filipe Thomaz identifies key themes of Manuel's imperial program: adopting an imperial title for the right of conquest, arrogating the right of navigation to the Indies and in the Indian Ocean, and claiming divine election for both king and people (Thomaz, "L'idee imperiale").[14] On the Iberian Peninsula, Portugal claimed territorial occupation but elsewhere "on unconquered territory" it exercised "eminent domination" in the form of tribute (38, my translation).

[14] On diplomatic relations with Ethiopia, see Aubin, "Duarte Galvão" and "L'ambassage."

Thomaz considers this strategy "Dom Manuel's crusade" (*la croisade*) with the keystone being "the destruction of the Islamic block": Manueline imperialism's "constant theme" was "the holy war" (50, 69).[15] Portugal cultivated diplomatic relations with African and Asian kings, such as Cochin and Kilwa, but non-European kings were always subordinate and used to repel Muslims.

Unsurprisingly, in a Manueline imperialism where the Portuguese are the elect, Pires is attentive to the intertwined categories of social class and race. Even the largest group of Christians in Asia, the Malabars, are racialized as "black" or "dark brown" (67). Dorothy Figueira argues that Pires "established an idyllic prelapsarian India where civilization is tied to social structures and long-standing membership in the Church" but racialized Indians through "skin colour and sexual impurity, or caste." (Figueira, "Race" 260–61). According to Figueira, Pires gives caste "moral dimensions," distinguishing the warrior caste of Nayars from the Brahmins by the latter's "purer blood" (68). He introduces a white/black distinction, noting such "white people" (48) as those in the Deccan of Turkish and Persian origin, the "white warriors from Persia" serving the lord of Chaul and Dande whose "father was a Turk by birth" (51), or the Chinese "white as we are . . . rather like Germans . . . The women look like Spanish women" (116–17). Even praise of China is treated skeptically, however, dismissed as "easier to believe as true of our Portugal than of China" (116). Evincing a burgeoning sense of Western superiority, Pires scorns the Chinese as "very weak and easy to overcome" (123). Such false dreams of easy conquest of China sent Pires on a disastrous embassy there.[16] However categorized, Asians are ultimately compared to an implied European normative, with Pires's analysis steeped in chivalric values.

2.2 Writing Southeast Asia

The dual foci on trade and religion also structure Pires's writing on Southeast Asia, dominating his work's second half. His emphasis on the eastern half of the Indian Ocean is evident in his chapter organization: Book 3 covers Bengal to Indochina, Book 4 China to Borneo, Book 5 focuses on the Indonesian Archipelago, and the work ends with Book 6 on Melaka. Bypassing places that are "not so profitable" (200), such as the islands between Java and the Moluccas, he focuses on important trading centers, expanding at length on their products, their peoples and culture, their religion, and even their history. The cultural information allows Pires to assess their receptiveness to trade with the Portuguese but also their vulnerability to conquest.

[15] Catz also detects "the spirit of the crusade" in Portuguese literature of expansion (Catz, "Consequences" 15).

[16] On Pires's failed embassy to China, see Pelliot, "Le Hōja."

Pires pays particular attention to a place's religious settlement. Some peoples are hostile to Muslims: he finds "very few Moors in Siam. The Siamese do not like them," though he somewhat contradictorily admits the presence of "Arabs, Persians, Bengalees, . . . and other nationalities" (104). The Moluccans are only superficially Muslims, "not very deeply involved in the sect," and often uncircumcised: "The heathen are three parts and more out of four" (213). Places with fewer Muslims are friendlier to the Portuguese. The island of Madura near Java has a "heathen" ruler, "no Moors and they [the islanders] are our friends" (228). Yet Muslim rulers can be allies. The sultan of Ternate welcomes "Christian priests," causing Pires to hope "if our faith seemed to him good he would forsake his sect and turn Christian" (215).

Along with a religious hierarchy, Pires makes civilizational distinctions between traders and non-traders. The relatively insignificant island of Laue, populated by "heathens," is declared "good" after he notes their diamonds, junks, gold, and merchants (225); moral goodness is equated with being "a good trading country" (225). Conversely, he racializes the inhabitants of the Amboina Islands: "It has people who are curly-haired, bestial; they have no merchandise. And they have not a very good port; they have no trade. It's a place for slothful people" ("*Hé jemte de cabello revolto, bestiall, nom tem mercadoria. E tem porto nom muito bom, nõ tem trato. Hé lugar de gemte priguosa*," 212; Loureiro 225). Lack of trading potential excludes a people from civilization and even renders them subhuman. Pires's modernity manifests in his rejection of travelers' tales from Pliny of "men with big ears who cover themselves with them" (222). However, in discarding medieval monsters, he institutes instead modern racial hierarchies.

Attention to civilizational markers yields Pires a wealth of information and he articulates several social elements that became part of modern anthropological writing on Southeast Asia. Among them is another civilizational distinction, the *hulu/hilir* (upstream/downstream) divergence, whereby riverine states rely on products from the resource-rich interior.[17] The wealth of coastal centers like Melaka depends on exerting political influence in the hinterland, though sometimes political power resides in the interior, but these relationships can turn sour. Pires notes this interior/coastal distinction for Pasai, Sumatra, which he says "has large towns with many inhabitants towards the interior, where important people of good breeding live. These sometimes disagree with Pase because of the crops of pepper, silk and benzoin; but they affirm that in the quarrels their wishes prevail over Pase" (143).

[17] This is first postulated by Bronson, "Exchange," a model later adopted by Drakard, *Malay Frontier*; Kathirithamby-Wells, "Hulu-Hilir Unity"; and Andaya, "Cash Cropping and Upstreams and Downstreams."

With the interior having the economic upper hand, Pires interprets its inhabitants' social standing as higher than coastal merchants, calling them "great nobles," "mandarins, and . . . men-at-arms" (143). In Pasai, a religious divergence also arises from coastal inhabitants increasingly converting to Islam. Coastal states are particularly cosmopolitan. While Pires would boast of the numerous nations flocking to Melaka, Pasai too is visited by "many merchants from different Moorish and Kling nations" (142). The inhabitants are mostly immigrants from Bengal, which sends junks annually to Melaka, such that even "natives descend from this stock" (142).

Trade motivates Pires's keen interest in political relations and history. Noting the state of persistent war, he repeats a local saying: "'Aru against Malacca, Achin against Pedir, Pedir against Kedah and Siam . . . and all these nations fight one against the other and they are very rarely friends" (147). He tracks close kin of ruling families: "The kings of Indragiri are related to the kings of Malacca and of Kampar and of Pahang" (153), information perhaps obtained from native sources. He also records historical details, such as the report that the founder of Melaka was named "Paramiçura" (158), or Parameswara in Malay sources, from Palembang in Sumatra, though the details of Melakan history are left to Book 6.

Pires's ethnographic writing depends not only on European observation but also on indigenous sources, though left unnamed. He retails local fables, such as the story of an island consisting wholly of women – "they have no men, and . . . they are got with child by others who go there to trade" – or the tale of "the enchanted queen in the hill of Malacca called Gunong Ledang" (162). The princess of Mount Ledang appears too in Malay chronicles, in the history of Melaka, *Sejarah Melayu*, and the prose romance *Hikayat Hang Tuah* discussed in Section 4. Pires explicitly acknowledges native sources for navigational knowledge: "If . . . I disagree with the pilots, it is not my fault, because in this I am relying on people who have been there; I have learnt this from Moors, from their charts [*suas cartãs*], which I have seen many times, and if their charts are not to be trusted, let it be clear that this should be for reading and not for navigation" (210–11; Loureiro 225). Local knowledges, including traditions of mapmaking deviating from European cartography, hybridize Pires's travel text. This hybridization is particularly evident in the extent of local historiography entering his book on Melaka.

2.3 Writing Melaka

Pires's travelogue ends with an extended dissertation on Melaka.[18] By first discussing parts further east, Pires conceptually shifts Melaka, "the end of the

[18] This section, however, is missing from the shorter, incomplete Lisbon manuscript.

monsoons," to the edge of the world (228). The final destination, Melaka, is the trading Jerusalem of the Indian Ocean. It anchors the imperial claims of the Iberians. As Ricardo Padrón shows, the Spanish "shift[ed] the antemeridian [of the 1494 Treaty of Tordesillas] eastward to Malacca" to map "the Castilian demarcation as a hemisphere stretching from the Marañon to Malacca, a transpacific space that included most of the New World along with East and Southeast Asia" (Padrón, *Indies* 34). This demarcation is in counterpoint to the Portuguese claim to the region from China to the Moluccas. Such a Portuguese claim underlies Pires's writing of Melaka. His historiography is admirably attentive to kingly succession, diplomatic relations, and political expansionism. As part of this larger claim, Pires, I argue, positions the Portuguese as successors to the Malay sultanate.

Pires's account forms a blueprint for the new rulers. The history of Melaka and an overview of its native governance constitute institutional knowledge to ensure continuity in the transition to Portuguese rule. Barbara and Leonard Andaya note, "Pires intended the *Suma Oriental* to be an authentic account of Melaka's history which could serve as a reference book for its new Portuguese masters" (Andaya and Andaya, *History of Malaysia* 34). His history's broad outline conforms to that of the major Malay chronicle, *Sejarah Melayu*:

> Both trace the Melaka line to an individual ruling in Palembang; both mention his special status; both describe his departure for Singapore, where he sets up a settlement. They relate how the settlement was later moved to Muar, about 8 kilometres from Melaka, then to Bertam, being finally established at Melaka itself, the site of which was chosen because of a mousedeer's peculiar behaviour. (Andaya and Andaya, *History of Malaysia* 34–35)[19]

Their divergence arises out of their different purposes. The Malay *Sejarah Melayu* is a genealogy of kings, not intended to be "strictly chronological" but rather for "the edification of future generations" (Andaya and Andaya, *History of Malaysia* 34). In contrast, Pires's reference book includes an account of trade and the legal system covering matters of taxation, licensing, the monetary system, weights and measures, and the like. His concluding section on the conquest shows how the Portuguese grafted themselves onto the port kingdom and its landscape.

Pires's historical research is not merely of antiquarian interest but also serves the colonial project of controlling and commanding an Asian population, both native inhabitants and foreign merchants. Although citing no specific source, he

[19] In Pires, it is a hare rather than a mouse deer that turns on the hunting dogs. Ferrand ("Malaka") argues for an earlier date for Melaka's foundation while Rouffaer ("Was Malaka emporium") suggests it was only established after 1400. On Islam's coming, see Wake, "Malacca's Early Kings."

shows evidence of absorbing native sources, whether directly or by transmission through Portuguese chroniclers, and credits native chronicles: "According to the Javanese, Malacca is said to be peopled in this way, which is set down in their chronicle and which is widely confirmed by them" (230). Despite Pires's error-ridden renderings of personal and place names, and while he may not have been able to read books in Javanese and Sundanese, Pires "accurately recorded many of the names and titles . . . , presumably from only hearing them spoken" (Noorduyn, "Concerning the Reliability" 468). Shaping his sources into a narrative, Pires makes the case for Portuguese rule.

Pires's differences from *Sejarah Melayu* reveal their disparate understandings of Melaka's place in the world. *Sejarah Melayu* sets Melaka in a global history, but Pires comprehends its history as regional. Its regionality makes Melaka discursively encompassable for incorporation into the Portuguese empire. Both texts trace the beginnings of Melaka to Palembang, but while *Sejarah Melayu* connects Palembang's royal house to a line of kings sired by Alexander the Great in India, Pire's framing casts Melaka as a breakaway tributary state of the Javanese empire and its growth as part of trading's ebb and flow.[20] Opening with the early history of Java from 1360, Pires casts Melaka's founder, Paramjçure (Parameswara), son of the king of Palembang, as a rebel. Married to the niece of the Javanese king and their tributary vassal, he revolts, calling himself "the Great Exempt" (231). Losing the war, Parameswara flees to Singapore, whose ruler he kills to become the new lord. When the assassinated ruler's father-in-law, the king of Siam, attacks Singapore, Parameswara retreats to Muar until invited to rule in Bentan by the inhabitants of Melaka, whom Pires calls "the *Celates*" (233).

Not only does Pires cast Parameswara as a rebel, he also others his supporters. A Portuguese neologism, the name Celates comes from the Malay word *selat*, meaning "strait," for those who inhabit that watery space, living off of its sea-bounty; in Malay they are known as *orang laut*, or sea people (Ferrand, "Malaka" 11:434). Parameswara's *translatio* conforms to that in *Sejarah Melayu*, though the Orang Laut ranged widely through the Riau Archipelago, as Pires acknowledged (233). He ascribes to them a sinister aspect, calling them "corsairs . . . who go out pillaging in their boats" and "robbers (who sometimes fished for their food)" (233). He notes their unchivalric combat methods in using poisonous blowpipes: "They carry blow-pipes with their small arrows of black hellebore which, as they touch blood, kill, as they often did to our Portuguese in the enterprise and destruction of the famous city of Malacca" (233). In this way Pires casts a shadow over Melaka's foundation.

[20] For the Alexander theme, see Ng, *Alexander the Great*, chapter 1.

Attending to how Melaka's rulers navigate political allegiances among the neighboring empires of Siam, Java, and China, Pires offers a history of a network in transition with Melaka's rise. In the time of Parameswara's son, Muhammad Iskandar Shah (Xaquem Darxa), Melaka grew from the flow of traders from Pasai, on the north coast of Sumatra, especially Muslim merchants, as well as people from other parts of Sumatra and the Riau Archipelago who "came to work" (241). It intercepted traffic from China to Pasai. Relations with Pasai led to conversion to Islam, as Iskandar Shah marries Pasai's daughter. Pires casts this, however, as coercion, blaming "mollahs" advising Pasai's king to "turn him [Iskandar Shah] away from his race and heathenry and to convert him, and this by underhand means and not publicly" (242). The dominant power, however, is China, which Iskandar Shah visits to "see the king to who Java and Siam were obedient" (242) and to whom he becomes a tributary vassal. He takes to wife the "beautiful Chinese daughter" (242) of the captain who brings him back – perhaps a reference to Ming admiral Zheng He, who made several voyages to the Indian Ocean, including stops in Melaka.[21]

Their son Raja Putih's progeny became kings of Pahang, Kampar, and Indragiri (243). Iskandar Shah strengthened his position by cultivating relationships with both Muslim merchants and China. The next king, Muzaffar Shah, embarked on an expansion of the kingdom by conquering nearby territories to annex their natural resources like tin, subduing places as far as Kedah and Singapore, and even warring on Sumatran kingdoms. This fame expanded Muzaffar Shah's network further: "he had messages and presents from the kings of Aden and Ormuz and of Cambay, and Bengal, and they send many merchants from their regions to live in Malacca" (245). This expanded network would be fictionalized into travel narratives of embassies from Melaka to India and the Middle East in *Hikayat Hang Tuah*, discussed in more detail in what follows.

Pires records how, as Melaka expanded, it became more cosmopolitan and welcoming, even assimilating several nations. The next king, Muzaffar Shah's son Mansur Shah, gave foreigners high positions at his court. He "raised men from nothing. The comptroller of his exchequer was a heathen Kling [South Indian Tamils], and they say he had such influence with him that he did nothing but what he wished; and in the same way a *Cafre* [kaffir] of Palembang who was his slave had such influence, that people said they were winning him back to his original heathenry" (249). The grandsons of both became powerful courtiers, one the *bendahara* (prime minister) and the other the *laksamana* (admiral).

[21] On Zheng He in Southeast Asia, see Wade, "Zheng He Voyages" and Wang, "Opening of Relations" and "China and Southeast Asia."

Mansur Shah also took as concubines "the beautiful daughters of Parsee merchants and the Klings" (249). He converted them to Islam and then "married them to mandarin's sons and gave them dowries" (249), marriages Pires identifies as mixed: "this custom of marrying people of different sects causes no surprise in Malacca" (249).

While Pires notes the Muslims' admiration for Mansur Shah, some of his characterizations are pointedly critical; he calls Mansur Shah "a gambler and luxurious" (249). Pires's critical remarks on Mansur Shah and his successor, Alauddin, focus on religion, with his suspicion of Islam, and opium as a mark of royal dissipation. Mansur Shah prepared for the Hajj in Mecca by amassing "a large amount of gold in a junk which he had ordered to be built in Java, and another in Pegu of great size," spending much money and gathering "many people for the journey" (250), though illness prevented the journey. His son Alauddin is similarly devout but also addicted to opium: "They say this king was more devoted to the affairs of the mosque than to anything else; and he was a man who ate a great deal of *afiam*, which is opium, and sometimes he was not in his right mind" (251).

Alauddin too made preparations for Mecca "to carry out his father's pilgrimage" but died before he could do so (251). The conjunction of pilgrimage and opium recalls Garcia da Orta's characterization of Sultan Bahadur, discussed in my Introduction. Pilgrimage to Mecca, a prominent aspect of Muslim trading networks, is viewed negatively. Even as Europeans were eager to discover new botanicals, they denigrated their rivals' consumption habits fostered by trade. Pires is particularly critical of the last king of Melaka, Mahmud, who he describes as "less just than any of the previous ones, very luxurious, intoxicated with opium every day" (253). He belabors Mahmud's lack of bodily control: "He was a great eater and drinker, brought up to live well and viciously" (253) and he kills his wife "just because the fancy came to him when he was intoxicated with opium" (254).[22]

Emphasizing Mahmud's "diabolical cruelty," Pires views his treatment of the Portuguese, namely the planned assassination of Captain Diogo Lopes de Sequeira, as being of a piece with his violence toward his courtiers (254).[23] True to form, Pires blames Muslim trading communities for prejudicing the king against the Portuguese: the Gujaratis, Arabs, Bengalis, and Tamils contend

[22] While also critical of Mahmud, *Sejarah Melayu* makes no mention of opium consumption, only depicting him as unjust and sexually voracious. When attending the wedding of the daughter of his prime minister (*bendahara*), Mahmud discovers her great beauty and becomes displeased that he was not informed of her beauty so he could marry her. Seizing on a pretext, Mahmud accuses the prime minister of fomenting revolt and has him executed before subsequently marrying Tun Fatimah (chapter 22).

[23] The first Portuguese fleet arrived on September 11, 1509.

that "besides robbing by sea and by land, they [the Portuguese] were spying in order to come back and capture it [Melaka], just as all India was already in the power of the Portuguese" (255), an accusation already made of Vasco da Gama and a repeated trope in Luís de Camões's epic poem *Os Lusíadas* (1572).

Bringing gifts, the merchants persuade various ministers to turn against the Portuguese: they "converted the *Bemdara* [Bendahara] to their plot" (255). However, the court is fractured. The Laksamana and Temenggung (chief of security) oppose this plot as the Portuguese "had come to his port in good faith" (256). The king's response reiterates accusations of spying that accompanied Portuguese arrival in the Indies:

> They come to spy out the land so that they can come afterwards with an armada . . . they go about conquering the world and destroying and blotting out the name of our Holy Prophet. Let them all die . . . we will destroy them on the sea and on the land. We have more people, junks, gold in our power than anyone else. Portugal is far away. Let them all be killed. (256)

The speech frames the encounter as a religious clash of civilizations. Portugal's distance underlines the arrivals' vulnerability while Melaka is a wealthy and formidable opponent. Moreover, the evil Bendahara forcefully converts the captured Portuguese and circumcises them, an act of violence that led to a death.

In contrast, *Sejarah Melayu* describes the first Portuguese fleet from Goa visiting without incident (*Sejarah Melayu* 254). The report of Melaka's wealth incites Afonso d'Albuerque's attack. The Portuguese are the aggressors. Yet, despite important differences, Pires's narrative of the Laksamana's opposition resonates with *Sejarah Melayu*'s account of his falling out of royal favor. *Sejarah Melayu* presents it as a problem of the king's bad advisors whose backbiting leads to Mahmud's tyrannical act of exiling his deeply loyal Laksamana, Hang Tuah; this narrative is repeated in the prose romance *Hikayat Hang Tuah*. The incident is unrelated to the Portuguese, though the Bendahara is similarly identified as Albuquerque's main opponent (*Sejarah Melayu* 255).

In Pires, the disagreement centers on the king's violation of guest-host relations: the Laksamana says, "This business is contrary to justice" ("*Este neguocio he comtra justiça*" 257; Loureiro 259). Mahmud's own injustice provokes Portuguese retaliation. Pires depicts the Portuguese as desiring peace but blocked by an obstinate king who "never wanted peace," surrounded by war hawks offering "to run completely amok for the king" ("*ao rey se faziam cabaeẽs amoquos*" 280; Loureiro 280). While the two texts apportion blame differently, notably both identify a schism in the court.

For Pires, the king is so unjust that even his admiral refuses to make war on the Portuguese. Growing suspicious of his power, the king murders the Bendahara, his sons, and his grandsons, stabbing them, as he did his wife, "with a kris" (258). This Malay weapon, a short dagger with a wavy blade, was becoming associated with running amuck (*amok*), the act of going on a killing frenzy that appeared irrational to Europeans (Batchelor, "Crying a Muck"). This early association of opium and running amuck would be enduring. Even an 1820 travel narrative critical of Dutch colonization vividly depicts the amok thus: "he . . . grips the snaked kris in his fist, and captured by the intoxicating power of bang, or opium, he first kills his torturer and runs then, his long jet-black hair waving wildly around his head" (Haafner, *Lotgevallen* 107, qtd. in Lefevere, "Composing the Other" 90). Already in Pires, the taking of opium is linked to uncontrolled violence. Accounts of native misrule justify Portuguese rule.

In his concluding section on the conquest, Pires praises the city – "Malacca is of such importance and profit that . . . it has no equal in the world" (285) – though not its former rulers. While the war was disruptive, Melaka is poised for a renaissance: "Malacca cannot help but return to what it was, and [become] even more prosperous" both because "it will have our merchandise" and because "we show them greater truth and justice" (283). Painting a picture of a port being rebuilt and its traffic increasing, he asserts, "A Solomon was needed to govern Malacca, and it deserves one" (283).

In speaking of Portuguese rule as a Solomonic destiny Pires frames the conquests as a millenarian fulfilment and Melaka as a new Jerusalem. Solomon's symbolic purchase for global trade and empire rests on the related biblical stories of the voyage he sent to Ophir for gold to build the first temple of Jerusalem and the embassy he received from the queen of Sheba (1 Kings 9:26–28, 10:11–15; 2 Chronicles 8:18, 9:21–27). This Solomonic theme would be further elaborated on by Manuel Godinho de Erédia, discussed next, and featured in other early modern European travel accounts.[24] The building of Melaka's fortress mimics the building of the temple, situated as it was on a sacred site, "on the site of the great mosque" (281) built by Mansur Shah, and thus displacing it. Instead of the "beautiful mosque" the Portuguese erected their "famous fortress" (249). For Pires, the destruction of Islam – "Mohammed will be destroyed" (286) – goes hand in hand with Portuguese control of global trade: "Whoever is lord of Malacca has his hand on the throat of Venice" (287).

[24] These include Portuguese Pedro Fernandes de Queirós, navigator for a Spanish voyage that discovered the South Pacific Solomon Islands, and Samuel Purchas in *Hakluytus Posthumus, or Purchas His Pilgrimes* (1625): see Sheehan, "Science and Patronage," and Sen, "Solomon, Ophir."

2.4 Conclusion

Portuguese presence in Asia constituted not a territorial empire but a discontinuous network. Noting the *Estado da Índia*'s hetereogeneity in a seminal 1985 article, Luís Filipe Thomaz influentially defines it not as a space but as a network of relations: "More than its discontinuous space (*descontinuidade espacial*) is the heterogeneity (*heterogeneidade*) of its institutions and the imprecision of its limits, both geographical and juridical, that makes it unusual . . . the *Estado da Índia* is in its essence a *network* (*rede*), that is, a system of communication (*um sistema de comunicação*) among various spaces" (Thomaz, "Estrutura" 208, my translation).

Building on Thomaz's acute observation of the "dispersion and variety of political regimes of territories" that made the Portuguese empire a "network" (*rede*) or matrix (*matriz*), António Manuel Hespanha's study of *mestiços* further contends that its "fluidity" (*fluidez*) derives "from the fact that an imperial network has been established on top of previous networks of other types, namely commercial networks, sometimes incompletely integrated into the 'empire' or constituting a non-political extension or complement of it that formed a kind of shadow" (Hespanha, *Filhos* 21, my translation).[25]

In other words, this discontinuous network intersected with a preexisting native network in the Indian Ocean. Pires's travelogue articulates the two to insert the Portuguese narratively into this prior system. He shows an antiquarian interest in local histories and is especially informed when it comes to the history of Melaka. But, while a keen observer, he also imports European frameworks to understand the Indian Ocean, particularly in his attention to race, religion, and social class. He shapes his historical materials to depict the last sultan as a violent opium addict. His narrative strategies are those of displacement and overlay. Just as the Portuguese fort in Melaka was built on the site of the great mosque, the Portuguese takeover caps his historical account. Imagining the Portuguese as successors to the Malay sultanate, Pires sees Portuguese destiny as a Solomonic one that would build a new trading Jerusalem in Melaka.

3 Erédia's Southern Imagination

The spatial imaginary of the earliest Portuguese eyewitness account of Melaka made the East quotidian and ordinary and thus suited for settlement. While Pires writes Melaka into the ultimate destination, Manuel Godinho de Erédia (1563–1623) views it instead as the beginning of exploration. Writing nearly a century later, Erédia was by his own account a *mestiço*, born in Portuguese Melaka and raised in a *casado* household. Leaving Melaka at thirteen, he furthered his

[25] Hespanha applies George Winius's term "shadow empire" to an empire that is "a loose constellation of quite autonomous and diverse groups" (Hespanha, *Filhos* 14, 16).

education at the Jesuit school in Goa, where he lived for much of his adult life. He would have been about thirty-eight years old when he returned to Melaka in 1601 for four years to pursue his project of discovery.

Erédia's penchant for exaggeration has led scholars to consider him "a (trans) cultural imposter, intellectual deceiver," one of the "trickster travelers leading double lives" and a "liar" (Flores, "Between Madrid" 184–85), or "an inordinately ambitious actor who was buffeted about by a set of realities about which he had little comprehension" (Subrahmanyam, "Between a Rock" 437).[26] Yet his maps are surprisingly modern, referencing Hokkaido before its nineteenth-century discovery by Europeans and correctly showing Korea as a peninsula (Gunn, *Imagined Geographies* 141).[27] Erédia's drive for patronage leads him to claim (an unproven) status as a royal cosmographer and the discoveries of new lands, including, most controversially, that of a southern land that might have been Australia.

Erédia's travel narratives draw on classical European as well as native sources. Sanjay Subrahmanyan notes the "mixed" character of his sources for Southeast Asian islands of gold, from Ptolemy and classical constructions of the Golden Chersonese to Malay legends, and "tales carried by Malay sailors and maritime communities (or *orang laut*)" (Subrahmanyam, "Between a Rock" 436). Even his mapmaking has been described as "hybrid" in that "he assimilated local knowledge in the way of boldly modifying Ptolemaic templates" (Gunn, *Imagined Geographies* 140–41). Erédia's compulsion to apply a classical Greco-Roman lens means fitting Asian spaces into a Ptolemaic or biblical frame and relating them to classical place names. In particular, he locates the biblical Solomon's Ophir, the source of gold, in Southeast Asia. At the same time, his use of native sources shows the cross-cultural circulation of travel narratives, in part even if not in whole.

In his self-fashioning as a discoverer, Erédia also understands discovery as a quest for new, unknown lands. His works display a tension between the notion of discovery as recovering something already known by the ancients and discovery as an accidental happening upon something not previously known. The latter usually comes about through the happenstance of storms throwing ships off course. Erédia uses the verb *desgarrar*, meaning to stray or to deviate. The waywardness inherent in the term suggests the errors and wanderings of the romance genre (Fuchs, *Romance* 64, 69). These episodes include many of romance's elements: a wandering (*desgarrando*), sometimes shipwreck, to end

[26] Subrahmanyam also terms him a "trickster" ("Between a Rock" 437; *Courtly Encounters* 116).

[27] For Erédia's cartographic contributions, whose charts influenced those of João Teixeira Albernaz I, see Alegria et al., "Portuguese Cartography" 997–1000, 1022–25.

in a miraculous discovery. Upon closer examination, however, despite the foregrounding of European explorers, such discoveries are often mediated by natives.

In what follows, I explore how Erédia straddles the European-native divide by examining three topoi of his cosmographical work: his re-spatialization of Melaka and its environs; his narratives of discoveries of islands of gold, including Solomon's Ophir; and, finally, the autobiographical account of his Sulawesian mother's voyage of escape, another romance narrative. Using both Greco-Roman and native sources, he rescripts the built environment and its social meanings to turn Melaka into a Portuguese city. If dominion in the East is Portugal's Solomonic destiny, his narratives of discovery nonetheless reveal how European knowledge must be supplemented with accidental discovery that depends on native knowledges. Hidden in his own autobiography is the figure of his native mother as a central agent.

3.1 Re-spatializing Melaka

What Jorge Flores notes about Erédia's work on the Mughal empire, *Discurso sobre a Provinçia do Indostan chamada Mogūl* (*Discourse on the Province of Hindustan Called Mughal*, 1611), holds true as well for his work on the Malay Archipelago: "The text is significant for the end result, but more so for the complex web of sources and influences that underpin it: texts from classical antiquity, Indo-Persian sources (both read and reported) and oral reports" (Flores, "Two Portuguese Visions" 63). Erédia liberally sprinkles his texts with classical citation but also reveals rudimentary knowledge of Konkani (in the vocabulary used for his botanical treatise), though he probably had greater fluency with Malay, with Malay sources and traditions likely accessed through oral sources (Flores, "Between Madrid" 186–87; Subrahmanyam, *Courtly Encounters* 114–15). Like Pires, he cites indigenous texts for the history of Melaka's foundation by Parameswara, alluding to "Malay annals" (*os annaes Malaios*) in his *Informação da Aurea Quersoneso* (*Report on the Golden Chersonese*, 1597–1600) (Mills 229; Caminha, 68).[28] Might his detailed history of Melaka have owed to a version of *Sulalat us-salatin* (*Sejarah Melayu*, or *The Malay Annals*)?

It has been argued that Erédia's contemporary, the Goa-based historian Diogo do Couto (ca. 1542–1616) possibly was familiar with *Sejarah Melayu* as he gives an account of Melaka's founding that differs markedly from the accounts

[28] Where Mills has translated the text (Erédia, "Eredia's Description"), I cite from his translation but also give citations to the Portuguese text; parenthetical citations are referenced by the editors' names; occasionally I silently revise the translation for clarity.

of other Portuguese writers, Pires, Barros, as well as Erédia. They tell of Melaka's founding by the refugee Parameswara who killed his host in Singapore and usurped the throne but then had to flee to escape an avenging relative, the Pahang king.

In contrast, Couto identifies Melaka's founder as the last sultan of Singapore, Iskandar Shah, who fled there after his treasurer betrayed the city to the Javanese kingdom of Majapahit in retaliation to the unjust punishment of his daughter, the king's concubine, wrongly accused of infidelity, a version closely adhering to *Sejarah Melayu* (Gibson-Hill, "Malay Annals"). Although Erédia's version conforms to the mainstream of Portuguese accounts, having spent much of his life in Goa, he knew Couto, who was the keeper of the Goa archives from 1595 to 1616 and collected both Portuguese and indigenous sources (Macgregor, "Johore Lama" 117).[29] He might have known of *Sejarah Melayu* and, even if he did not have access to Couto's personal library, as a student at the Goan Jesuit school, he would have had access to their library. His use of a variety of sources, including non-Western and local ones, replicates Couto's methods.

Although *Sejarah Melayu* most immediately invites comparison, Erédia's details on Sumatra also suggest possible access to a roughly contemporaneous Sumatran chronicle from Aceh, *Hikayat Aceh*.[30] He notes how in Perlak, Aceh, "has been discovered [*se descobrirão*] the unceasing springs of Earth Oil … called 'Minsat Tanna' [*minyak tanah*]" (Mill 238; Caminha 96–97) in quantities to supply lamp oil for the east coast. *Hikayat Aceh* shows petroleum (*minyak tanah*) as one of two products – the other is camphor – sought after by the Turkish embassy, suggesting its importance to Aceh's international trade (91). The other similar detail is the reference to "a salt-water lake containing an astonishing number of 'Taynha'-fish" in Sumatra's interior (Mills 238; Caminha 97). In *Hikayat Aceh*, a hilltop lake in the interior, inhabited by fantastical creatures and oceanic fish, appears in a self-ethnography attributed to the Turkish embassy (94).

The interweaving of Greco-Roman and native sources undergirds Erédia's discursive effort to revamp a Malay city into a Portuguese one. For the most part, there was considerable continuity between Malay and Portuguese Melaka. While there were some shifts in the social hierarchy of the merchant communities, Luís Filipe Thomaz considers the change to be "hardly profound" (Thomaz, *Malaka* 43, my translation), though Paulo Pinto traces the city's

[29] For a reconstruction of Couto's library, see Loureiro, *Biblioteca*.

[30] While Braginsky ("Structure") dates it to circa 1607–36, Iskandar (*Hikayat Aceh* xlviii–lii) argues for its composition by the Sufi sheikh Syamsuddin of Pasai, active in Aceh when Sir James Lancaster arrived in 1602.

transformation with the center of power shifting to the *casados*, especially the captain of Melaka as part of an administrative machine (Pinto, *Portuguese* 187–203). The result was a creolization: a "creole port city," Fernando Rosa argues, uncovers the "multilayered, ancient, and . . . complex . . . movements of people across" the Indian Ocean (Rosa, *Portuguese* 10).

However, while creolization implies an organic process of creative fusion, I emphasize the forceful, even violent, reshaping of native forms, especially in their reception by the indigenous population. For the stones of the destroyed principal mosque "were reused for the construction of the fortress *A Famosa*, which took its place" (Thomaz, *Malaka* 43). The architectural transformation of the city defines an inside and an outside, a segmentation that enforces social and racial boundaries.

The Portuguese fort is highlighted as Melaka's most prominent architectural feature in Erédia's description in *Declaraçam de Malaca e Índia Meridional com o Cathay* (*Description of Melaka and Meridional India and Cathay*, 1613).[31] *A Famosa* continues to this day to be a sightseeing attraction, though now in ruins. It is the first thing Portuguese installed to change the landscape of their new conquest. António Hespanha places Portuguese Melaka in "the model of empire centered on the dominion of fortresses (*fortalezas*) . . . but it is key to a vast space" as "one of the most cosmopolitan commercial centers" (Hespanha, *Filhos* 151, my translation). Rather than on top of a hill, the fort is built at its foot. Its location by the sea makes reinforcements for war easy. But the fort's placement must also be seen in relation to the past government: it was "the same spot where Sultan Muhammad had his palaces and kept the treasure with which he retired up the river" (Mills 17; Janssen 4). The Portuguese planted themselves *in place of* the old Malay order.

The old palace is transformed into a military installation to enforce order. Rather than the wood of native construction, the fort is built of longer-lasting "stone and mortar" (Mills 17; Janssen 4). Supplied by a well in the middle, the quadrilateral fort is sufficiently spacious to shelter people from the surrounding countryside in the event of a siege. Despite delays and other problems with fortifying the city – lacking strong walls even on the eve of a Dutch siege in 1605, with the walls completed only in the 1630s (Pinto, *Portuguese* 216, 218–19) – nonetheless, Erédia, I suggest, understands the fort as symbol to project Portuguese imperial might (and violence) onto the local inhabitants:

> After the fortress had been finished and stood complete with its artillery and garrison of soldiers, it created among the Malays a feeling of intense dread

[31] In this regard, he departs from Pires, in whose time the fort would not yet have been completed.

> and astonishment [*muyto terror e espanto*] which lasted permanently to the great credit and honour of the Crown of Portugal. (Mills 17; Janssen 5)

Much has been made of how Eastern marvels elicited wonder in Europeans and conversely how European technology – exemplified by Stephen Greenblatt's "invisible bullets" (*Shakespeare Negotiations* 36–39) – overawed and amazed natives. Less has been said about colonial affects not stemming from native incomprehension.

Applying Sianne Ngai's "ugly feelings" to the project of decolonization, Neetu Khanna argues for a set of political feeling or visceral logics arising from anticolonial struggles (Ngai, *Ugly Feelings*; Khanna, *Visceral Logics*). Extending this argument, I suggest that colonization too has its visceral logics. Portuguese Melaka's imposing fort, made of uncommon material and "as high as the hill" (Mills 17; Janssen 5), was intended to evoke colonial dread. This affect marks the efficacy of imperial imposition. The "great credit and honour" come from the fortress's impermeability: "For the fortress was attacked time and again by the Malayo Kings and other neighbouring peoples, it always proved victorious" (Mills 17; Janssen 5). Erédia would not have known that, three decades later, in 1641, it would fall to a joint attack by Johor (where the exiled Melaka court reestablished itself) and the Dutch. It was sufficient that it had stood for a century.

The fort or tower is the start, not the end, for the reshaping of the surrounding lands. The country's boundaries are defined by walls: ramparts of stoneworks separate shore from the city, with additional earthern ramparts to surround seaside suburbs. Although these defend from sea attacks, in practice the population will move into the fortress. While previously the ill-defined boundaries of town and country allow for Melaka's easy interaction with the sea peoples and inhabitants of the upcountry, the newly erected walls and ramparts now control the flow of peoples through gates that "pierced" the walls, with two "in common use and open for traffic," with one by the customs house (Mills 18; Janssen 6). Within the walls, additional buildings house peculiarly Portuguese institutions: administrative government buildings, churches, hospitals, and a charity house. The city becomes a European walled city with a tower keep.

Physical segmentation of the landscape with stone and earthenworks visibly delineates social categories and distinctions. The core contains Portuguese stone buildings for the governors; outside but within earthen ramparts separating land from sea are the suburbs inhabited by Malays and other non-Europeans. The housing of communities by ethnic group is inherited from their Malay predecessors, but now the stone fort defines a center where Portuguese-affiliated groups concentrate: "The Portuguese, the mixed race (*métis*) or assimilated (*assimilés*), settled mainly in the center of the city, around the fortress and the church, which have replaced respectively the mosque and the sultans' palace" (Thomaz, *Malaka* 44, my translation).

Moreover, the villages (Malay *kampung*) are denoted parishes and given names of Christian saints, though Erédia also identifies them by their former names. "Campon Chelim" (*kampung Keling*, or Indian village), where "live the Chelis of Choromandel," seems more homogenous, while "Campon China" (*kampung Cina*, or Chinese village) is a mixed community of "Chicheos, descendants of the Tochâros of Pliny, and stranger merchants and native fishermen," but both, located within the most prominent suburb outside the walls, as well as parishes in other suburbs all contain Christians and "infidel natives" (Mills 19; Janssen 5–6). These Christians are native converts, for the Portuguese *casados* (married men), who number 300, and their families live within the fortress garrison.

Erédia's social taxonomy categorizes peoples outside of Melakan political society as barbaric. They constitute two major groups: the people of the sea and those of the forest. The first group he designates "a fisher-folk, the 'Saletes,'" as did Pires:

> These fishermen employed pointed darts called "*soligues*" [*seligi* in Malay, spearheads made of sharpened bamboo], with which they transfixed the fish swimming at the bottom of the sea: they used no other devices for catching fish. They were a wild, cannibal race, who inhabited the coast of Ujontana in the southern sea. (Mills 16; Janssen 4)

Their primitiveness is marked by the simplicity of their tools: spearing fish is slower and the catch of a lower volume. The othering of the *selates* by stereotyping them as cannibals separates them decisively from Melakan civility. This boundary-marking departs from other European descriptions. In Pires, they are robbers and pillagers, not cannibals. The trader Jacques de Coutre describes them as poor fishermen, though treacherous:

> Many fishermen live along these straits, who are called *saletes* ... They are extremely poor people. They live in sloops that are five or six varas long at most, and are very narrow, made of thin, light planks, and on them they have their houses with wives and children, dogs, cats and even hens with their chicks ... They are treacherous people by nature. (Coutre, *Memoirs* 77)

Their watery homes are also described by Peter Mundy, who in the "old straightt" of Singapore (Selat Tebrau) "saw sundry companies of small boates covered over with Mattes, which is the Ordinary habitation of those that live among these Ilands, Where they have their wives, children and Household goods" (Mundy, *Travels* 146–47). Describing them using "Fishgaes," he adds that "They use allsoe nets, hookes and lynes" (Mundy, *Travels* 146–47). While some Europeans viewed the *selates* as pirates, others only note their unusual fishing method (harpooning) and habitat (floating houseboats), considering these simply as ethnic customs rather than as civilizational markers.[32]

The *selates* fit well in the category of what Michael Pearson calls "littoral society," the "fisherfolk [who] live on shore, but work on the sea" (Pearson, "Littoral Society" 356).[33] Such communities are found across the Indian Ocean from the East African Swahili (a word that means "shore folk") to the Sama-Bajau sea nomads of Sulawesi. While littoral society is distinct from the port cities, as Jans Heesterman says, "The littoral forms a frontier zone that is not there to separate or enclose, but which rather finds its meaning in its permeability" (Heesterman, "Littoral" 89; qtd. in Pearson, "Littoral Society" 356). The *selates* or Oang Laut forming the littoral society of the Melaka Strait and Riau Archipelago were intimately connected with the port kingdom of Melaka. Before the Portuguese conquest, they served as a defensive force for Melaka's Malay rulers. Tomé Pires notes that Orang Laut had held the role of *laksamana*, or admiral, since Melaka's founding (235). They were well positioned to guard the maritime trade lanes with their intimate knowledge of the seascape. Even after Portuguese conquest when the court moved to Johor, they continued to play this role for the transplanted kingdom and were key players in the seventeenth-century war between Johor and Jambi in Sumatra.[34]

In their role as naval defense (or offense), the *selates* constituted a threat to Portuguese Melaka. Hence Erédia's racial othering of the *selates*, especially when compared to the forest dwellers. While historical evidence suggests that Parameswara founded Melaka through the support of the Orang Laut forces belonging to the Bentan king of Riau-Lingga, Erédia construes them as the original inhabitants displaced by Melaka's founding. His version sets them in opposition to Parameswara: "Before the foundation of the town, the place was inhabited by a fisher-folk, the 'Saletes,' who gathered in the shade of the myrobalan trees" (Mills 16; Janssen 4).[35] In *Sejarah Melayu*, the tree marks the spot: Melaka's founder, Iskandar Syah, seeing a fine location where a river meets the sea, is standing under a tree when his hunting dog is attacked by a white deer (*pelanduk putih*, 120); he names the place Melaka after the tree. Erédia therefore begins his account of Melaka with an etymology of the name,

[32] For their characterization as pirates, see Bowrey, *Geographical* 237.

[33] See also Emmerson, "Case," which applies to Southeast Asia the ideas of anthropologist Smith, *Those Who Live*.

[34] On Melaka's symbiotic relationship with Orang Laut, see Andaya, *Leaves*, 177, 186; on their role in the Johor-Jambi war, see Andaya, *Kingdom of Johor*, 90–93.

[35] L. Andaya, *Kingdom of Johor*, 45–51; O. W. Wolters, *The Fall of Srivijaya in Malay History* (Ithaca: Cornell University Press, 1970), 10, 12–13.

the fruit of which he identifies as a "myrobalan," defined by *Hobson-Jobson* as "[a] name applied to certain dried fruits and kernels of astringent flavour, but of several species ... exported from India, and had a high reputation in the medieval pharmacopoeia" (Yule, *Hobson-Jobson* 607–08). Disputing Barros's account, which conforms to Pires as discussed in Section 2, John Crawfurd asserts that the name must derive from "the Malaka plant, Phyllanthus emblics, ... abundant in the locality" (Crawfurd, *Descriptive Dictionary* 243). If the tree is symbolic of possession of the land, it is a transferable one. The continued occupation of the *selates*'s coastal home, however, means that the profitable maritime trade routes are contested.

The dynamic with the forest aborigines, whom Erédia calls "Banuas," shares similarities but also evinces differences. The name likely derives from the Malay word *benua*, originally Sanskrit, meaning the earth. A British colonial officer, Frank Swettenham (1850–1946), the first resident general of the Federated Malay States, calls them "Orang Benua," meaning the people of the country, in passages quoting from Erédia (Swettenham, *British Malaya* 26, 30). While Erédia also classifies them as savage – calling them "a race as wild (*agreste*) as the satyrs of Pliny" – he seems to admire their esoteric knowledge:

> These Banuâs are soothsayers like the soothsayers of Thuscia and live on the mountain called Gunung Ledang [Mount Ledang], where dwelt the Queen Puteri [princess], a magician and enchantress like the Thessalian Erichtho, who, by the medicinal virtues of herbs and plants, turned women into the shapes of tigers and other animals and birds. (Mills 23; Janssen 11)

Erédia's classical comparisons associate the Banuas not simply with wildness but also with divinity. As woodland gods, the satyrs are both divine and bestial in their quadrupedalism, part horse (or sometimes part goat) and part human.

The Banuas are distinguished by knowledge, particularly medical. Erédia himself, after all, wrote a herbal handbook, *Suma de árvores e plantas da Índia Intra Ganges* (*Summary of the Trees and Plants of India Intra Ganges*, 1612). In their intellectual pursuits, they are distinguished not only from the *selates* but also from the Malays. The Malays are described as "cheerful, roguish, and very wanton: ingenious and intelligent, but negligent and careless about studies and arts: they spend their time amusing themselves, and so, as a rule, few literati, mathematicians, or astrologers are to be found amongst them" (Mills 31; Janssen 21).

In contrast, though "wild," Banuas are "the most diligent of the people" in "devot[ing] themselves to learning magic arts in the caves of Gunung Ledang, as men did in the Phythian caves, acquiring proficiency in effecting witchcraft and sorcery. As herbalists, too, they disclose the virtues of the medicinal plants and herbs to the more curious of the Malays" (Mills 40; Janssen 32). Botanical and medicinal knowledges are conflated with magic. But classical comparisons to worship of the prophetic deity Apollo, also associated with medicine, make the Banuas more familiar.

Paradoxically, then, the wilder Banuas are defined as respectable pagan sources of knowledge. Firmly anchored in a specific geographical space, their locus, Ledang Mountain, is also given classical comparisons: there is "a certain cavern, like those Pythian and Sybilline caves, where the wild Banuas learn the medicinal arts, and hold communication with the devil in the dark caverns, where, without their seeing anyone, they hear the voice which reveals the virtues of the miraculous medicinal plants and herbs, as well as the methods of preparation and the proportions of component substances which are effectual for producing different results, beneficial and harmful" (Mills 41; Janssen 32). Finally, they are an organized community with "apprentices" who "act as doctors" (Mills 47; Janssen 37).

Erédia's account of Banuan magic, however, is not simply orientalist fantasy. The magical properties of their ruler, are in fact part of local legends about the Puteri Gunung Ledang (princess of Mount Ledang) and recounted in Malay chronicles. Indeed, one of Erédia's anecdotes about India that most strains credulity bears similarities to the animistic practices described in *Hikayat Hang Tuah*, discussed next: a *yogi* from the Gujarati hinterlands tells of a magician who "kept two black dogs by him, and these dogs would take the form of tigers when he so ordered to guard and protect his person" (*Documentação* 3:138; trans. and qtd. in Flores, "Distant Wonders" 573). *Hikayat Hang Tuah*'s protagonist studies magic with a mountain sage, is adept at using pharmaceuticals, and can transform himself into animals, including a tiger. While much of the Banuas' characterization appear to be exoticizations, as Jorge Flores reminds us, magical thinking was also widespread in Europe.

Erédia vacillates between projecting a *terra nullius* and mapping the terrain according to indigenous categories. Refusing to recognize the *selates*'s traditional possession of the coast, he argues from Melaka's absence in Ptolemy's *Geography* that it is a new city, asserting that "there were no human habitations on the site of Malaca" even while conceding that "the Saletes lived in their boats along the beaches of this coast" (Mills 23; Janssen 13). The Banuas are more readily accorded territorial dominion of the upland forest, well away from the coastal strip claimed by the Portuguese. In contrast, the Malays and other traders in Melaka are firmly incorporated, residing as they do under Portuguese control.

The Portuguese tried to convert the inhabitants to assimilate them into the new city. Portuguese self-insertion into the old Malay order is best seen in their integration of officials from the previous administration. The Malay sultanate's *bendahara*, or prime minister, and his family turned Christian and became loyal to the new rulers: "from then until now their house has shown great loyalty to the State and to the Christian religion: and at the present day his son the faithful Dom Fernando serves in this same office of *Bendahara*" (Mills 53–54; Janssen 42). Nor was the administrative class the only one to be co-opted. So were others who run the economy: "Moreover, baptism was accorded to many Chelis, merchants and farmers, some of whom were worth 10 or 12 '*bares*' of gold, and to many natives and strangers" (Mills 53–54; Janssen 42). The administrative class provided continuity in governance, even as conversion cut across a large swathe of society.

Erédia does not simply tell Melaka's history but adds to it, depicting the Portuguese as the new successors. The Portuguese rescript the city by transforming its architecture and by creating new boundaries between city and forest. They also, importantly, co-opt the inhabitants by converting them. Melaka is the beachhead from which the Portuguese launched missionary efforts to convert natives in further islands, including the Spice Islands, from which Erédia's mother came.

3.2 Solomon's Ophir and the Accidents of Discovery

In his persistent turn to antiquity, Erédia draws a link between Southeast Asia and the biblical King Solomon's Ophir. For early modern Europeans, Solomon's traffic with a series of Asian places – Ophir, to which he sent an embassy led by his friend, Hiram, king of Tyre, and which sent return fleets; Tarshish or Tharsis, whose fleets accompanied those of Ophir; and Sheba whose queen visited Jerusalem – became symbolic of global trade.[36] Earlier Iberian discoveries were linked to Solomon, starting with Christopher Columbus, who overlaid biblical sites onto his New World discoveries, identifying Hispanola (now Haiti and the Dominican Republic) first as Cipangu (Japan) and then as Solomon's Ophir, with its gold mines, making as well copious references to Tarshish (Flint, *Imaginative Landscape* 123–30).[37] Erédia's sources overlap with Columbus's, and not just the Bible but also Josephus's account of Solomon's fleet to Ophir (Mills 235; Flint 62), and he evinces the same fascination with Ophir and Tarshish, the subjects of his *Tratado Ophirico* (1616). An imperial theme shared not only with the Iberians but also other Europeans, the

[36] For passages on Ophir, Sheba, and Tarshish, see 1 Kings 9:22, 26–28, 10:11–15; 2 Chronicles 8, 9; Psalms 71:10–11.

[37] The introduction to Erédia's *Tratado Ophirico* discusses the range of places identified as Ophir and Tharsis (Gil and Loureiro 38–86).

Solomonic link allows Erédia to fashion a prophetic role for the Portuguese in the East Indies.[38]

In *Informação da Aurea Quersoneso*, Erédia identifies a place at the isthmus of the Malay Peninsula as Ophir, suggesting that the port Tana Sorir or Sorin, whose name means the land of Sorir, a kind of grass, may well be "the ancient port of Sophir mentioned by ... Josephus" both because "the Golden Chersonese has always been the land of Gold" and "the difference between the names is slight, and the pronunciation almost identical" (Mills 235; Caminha 88). Tana Sorir's location makes it a convenient "meeting-place of numerous merchants from Alexandria, Gujarat, Cambay, Hindustan, and other eastern nations, because of the gold and spices, which are always vented there, by way of the people of the Sumatran Peninsula, Java, Banda, and Makassar" (Mills 235; Caminha 89).

Erédia insists that Solomon's gold came from the India of the East (India Oriental) and not from Peru, a topic to which he returns repeatedly (Mills 235; Caminha 89). *Declaraçam de Malaca e da India Meridional com Cathay*, addressed to Philip of Spain, describes not just Melaka, but also a range of places from the distant to the fanciful: Cathay, Hindustan, and Turkestan, along with the Land of Darkness and the Desert of Demons, with a chapter on Ophir and Tharsis (Mills 80–81; Janssen 70–72). Here his geography is more exploratory, though he dismisses the New World (Hispaniola, Peru) or African (Sofala) hypotheses for Ophir. He traces the probable route of Solomon's fleet to the Ganges and shores it up with Ptolemy's recognition of a maritime network extending from the Red Sea to India and beyond to the Malay Peninsula and China as well as a land route across Persia. In *Informação*, Erédia even draws a chronological parallel by dating the ancient beginnings of Sumatra's Minangkabau kingdom to the time Solomon built the temple of Jerusalem (Mills 239; Caminha 98–99).

Tratado Ophirico repeats and expands on this earlier material. The first part treats Tharsis and Ophir; the second recounts Solomon's voyages, including to Ophir; and the third describes Asia from the Euphrates to Tartaria. As in *Declaraçam*, Erédia's sources are Josephus and Ptolemy. However, while he previously identifies Tana Sorir as Ophir, here he proposes two Ophirs with chapters on the India Major of Ophir (Hindustan, on the Indian subcontinent) and the India Minor of Ophir, which is Southeast Asia, just as he claims two Prester Johns, one in Africa and one in Asia (Gil and Loureiro 115). As the modern editors of *Tratado Ophirico* note, Erédia's attempt at reconciling

[38] On Samuel Purchas's framing of English East Indies voyages as their Solomonic destiny, see Sen, "Solomon, Ophir."

biblical and classical narratives with modern geographical information available in Goa frequently results in confusion (Gil and Loureiro 115n347).

Erédia's rejection of New World possibilities for Ophir, proposed largely by Spanish explorers, suggests Portuguese loyalties, though he wrote during the dynastic union of Spain and Portugal, from 1580 to 1640, dedicating his works to the reigning Spanish monarch. Discussing the division of the world in *Informação*, he insists on Portugal's right to the Maluku Islands "by law of priority" (Mills 248; Caminha 128). After Melaka's conquest, says Erédia, Alfonso d'Albuquerque ordered an expedition led by "Cosmographer" Antonio de Abreu, who "took possession of them in the name of the King Dom Manoel of Portugal on the twenty-fifth of April, 1503 [November 1511]" staking his claim with "[e]ngravings cut . . . on the Cliffs and Rocks of Maluku [Islands], representing the happy Arms of the Crown of Portugal," and thus Portugal has "ancient dominion . . . anterior to that of Spain" (Mills 248; Caminha 127–28). Although Abreu indeed came before Ferdinand Magellan's Spanish-backed voyage, Erédia transposes the dates of Melaka's conquest and Abreu's voyage to nearly a decade earlier. Featuring the heraldic arms of Portugal, legible largely only to Europeans, this ceremony of possession was aimed at Spanish rivals, as is Erédia's retelling.

Describing Abreu's purpose to be "to discover the famous Maluku Islands" (*a fim de descobrir aquellas famosas Ilhas Malucas*) (Mills 247; Caminha 127), Erédia exemplifies the definition of discovery as a recovery of what is suspected to be there. While waiting to be discovered, the Maluku Islands were already famous. This sense fits his representation of Southeast Asia as Ophir: Ophir's discovery is the recovery of ancient links to Solomon. Yet his texts are also replete with narratives of accidental discovery that depart from this model. In this significant strand, storms and shipwreck lead to the discovery of genuinely new lands. However, not only are these discoveries never in the first person, but also they are often mediated by native agents. Such accounts share a common sequence of events: (i) an accident, most often a storm, leading to an encounter; (ii) a relation by an informant; and (iii) Erédia's attempt at authentication with documents, often generated upon his instigation. The post-discovery work of documentation serves as substitute for an absent ancient attestation.

Erédia's *Informação* notes a number of such discoveries, particularly of ships blown off course and encountering strangers. The discoverers are not only Europeans but also non-Europeans. Erédia relates how Antonio Rodrigues de Luna, who "met with a storm [*com temporal*]," and Antonio Dias Sumatra were sailing along the western coast of Sumatra when they encountered Black men (*os Negros*) selling gold (Mills 240; Caminha 104). He mentions Nakhoda Timanaique of Masulipatam, on the eastern coast of India, "driven by a storm from the point of Gale [*com temporal desgarrou da ponta de Gale*] from Ceylon towards the Equinoctial line, where he visited an Island of gold" (Mills 241; Caminha 105).[39] The straying of the boat – described with the verb *desgarrar* – is underlined by the romance element of the prospect of gold.

But it is in *Declaraçam* that we find the most important example of discovery initiated by an event of *desgarrando*, or errant straying, that is the land of Luca Antara, constituting the work's second part. After discovering a chart by Erédia in 1861, British Library map librarian Richard Henry Major identified Luca Antara as Australia, but he later repudiated this claim to promote instead his friend John Crawfurd's surmise that it was simply Madura or another island in the Archipelago (Major, *Discovery of Australia* and "Further Facts").[40] As the initial claim is for Portuguese priority in contradistinction to the Dutch claim for Australia's discovery, the debate is Eurocentric.[41] Although Erédia gives himself the title of discoverer (*descobridor*, Mills 64; Janssen 54), he was unable to travel to Luca Antara due to illness. Instead, he relies on the eyewitness accounts of the king of Demak, Chiaymasiouro, and of his own servant.

The discovery is also initiated by an errant boat, though this time it is the strangers who find themselves "carried out of [their] course by storms and currents" to Java: "by the just decision of God, by chance [*a caso*] a boat from Lucaantara in Meridional India strayed with the storm and currents [*com temporal e correntes desgarrada*], came to land on the beach, and arrived at the port of Balambuam in Java Major" (Mills 61; Janssen 51). This event is random, happening by chance, but it is also divinely ordained. Erédia's description of the strangers wavers between the familiar and the new, comparing them to the Bantenese but also categorizing them as a new type: "These strangers from Lucaantara in build and cast of countenance, and of the rest resembled the Jaos [Javans] of Banten; but they spoke a different language: thus showing that they were Jaos of another type" (Mills 62; Janssen 51).

It is the local inhabitants who recognize them to be truly strangers and the Javanese prince who is the discoverer; Erédia merely reports: "This unusual incident [*esta novidade*] greatly excited the Jaos of Balambuan and their

---

[39] Nakhoda (*necoda*) is a word of Persian origin meaning captain.

[40] The English translator, Mills, however, offers several arguments against Crawfurd's identification: that a voyage to Madura would have been conducted against prevailing monsoon winds; that a prince of Demak would be recognized in Madura, making it an unlikely place for a voyage of discovery; that Eredia's servant Pedro de Carvalhaes notes the news made it to Surabaya and that Surabayans would detect any fraud since the closest distance between Surabaya and Madura is but a mile; and that Madura, at one-thirtieth the size of Java, is simply too small (Mills 189). Intriguingly, Erédia's maps show a southern continent (Gunn, *Imagined Geographies* 142).

[41] In 1606, Willem Janszoon, leading a Dutch East India Company exploratory voyage to New Guinea, sailed along its southern coast and landed in northern Queensland (Serle, "Willem Janszoon").

satraps, especially Chiaymasiouro, king of Demak [*Damuth*]; which by his curiosity [*sua coriosidade*], prince that he was, wished to venture [*aventurar*] for this discovery [*descobrimento*] of Lucaantara" (Mills 62; Janssen 51). The language of discovery emphasizes newness and the discoverer is a Javanese prince, whose nobility and desire to venture are framed in chivalric terms. The next year, the adventurous king of Demak made the voyage to this new land of Luca Antara – that is to say, Nusa Antara, *nusa* meaning island, *antara* meaning another or across – in a twelve-day sailing. Upon return, the king of Demark sent a letter to the king of Pahang, included in Erédia's text as an authenticating document:

> Having equipped myself for travel and supplied myself with necessary requirements, I embarked with some companions in a "*caletus*" or vessel provided with oars, and set out from the port of Balambuan towards the south. After a voyage lasting 12 days, I reached the port of Lucaantara; there I disembarked and was received by the *syahbandar* [harbor master] with demonstrations of pleasure. Being fatigued with the voyage, I was unable to see the King of Lucaantara, who was staying up-river in the Hinterland, eight days' journey away. (Mills 63; Janssen 52–53)

This report reveals familiar East Indies elements, namely the presence of a port with a harbor master with the king residing up stream. Such a pattern of encounters – a reception by the harbor master before proceeding inland to the court – is found in the embedded travel accounts of *Hikayat Hang Tuah*, discussed in the next section.

If the encounter replicates indigenous – or rather, Indian Ocean – patterns of travel to a foreign land and their narratives, the rest of the brief letter resembles a European ethnographic report in miniature. Reporting hospitable entertainment, Chiaymasiouro notes the fineness of the climate, gives a few details about the products of the country – notably gold but also spices – and comments on the people, their language, and their customs. His ethnography, moreover, takes the Javanese as the point of comparison:

> The people are Jaos, as in our own Java, though their language is somewhat different. They wear their hair hanging as far as the shoulder, while the head is girt with a fillet of hammered gold. The *keris* [wavy short sword] is ornamented with precious stones, like the *keris* with the curved scabbard in Bali.
>
> Speaking generally, the Jaós of Lucaantara spend their whole time in sports and pastimes: they are especially addicted to cock-fighting. (Mills 63; Janssen 53)

Eredia repeats the first sentence in this passage over and again in his *Declaraçam* and in his *Informação* but seems less interested in the details of the strangers' costume or pastimes that Chiaymasiouro relates. The customs – use of hammered gold, the wearing of the *keris*, and cockfighting – map well onto Javanese ones but not onto Portuguese.

Erédia tries to fit the new discovery into old patterns. Lacking ancient attestation, he creates modern ones of his own. Chapter 1 of part 2 narrates the strangers' arrival from Meridional India – that is, southern India, by which Erédia means a land to the south of Java. Chapter 2 gives the transcription of Chiaymasiouro's letter. Not content with this document, Erédia provides in chapter 3 a certificate from the Melakan alderman Pedro de Carvalhaes to certify having met with Chiaymasiouro and to confirm the letter's relations, even to the point of redundancy by repeating the contents word for word.

There is a tension in the narrative between the familiar and the new. Even as chance storms throw up new discoveries, Erédia places this southern land in relation to what is already known, whether geographically – noting how Luca Antara and Chile are each other's antipodes – or racially, remarking how the new land contains the "same variety of races, white, brown, and black, as is found in Europe, Asia, and Africa" (Mills 65; Janssen 54). While the whiteness of the people Erédia focuses on may well be due to the white body paint used by Australian aboriginals, it also speaks to Erédia's frame of mind that seeks the familiar. Thus, chapter 6, "De Descobrimento a Caso" ("Concerning Accidental Discoveries"), recycles legends, telling of an island of Amazons whose husbands are kept on a separate island, attested, Erédia claims, by "the annals and *lontars* [palm-leaf manuscripts] of Java" (Mills 66; Janssen 54). Where he lacks Greco-Roman classical or biblical attestations, Erédia looks for native ones.

Errant straying, despite its potential associations with chivalric romance, is not confined to Europeans. Natives, whether southern strangers, or Southeast Asians from the Indonesian Archipelago, are also caught up in the storms of fortune. The arrival of southern strangers prompting Chiaymasiouro's travel is doubled by a second appearance of a Luca Antara boat "driven out of its course by the currents [*desgarrada com correntes*] to arrive in Banda with white women [*molheres brancas*]" (Mills 66; Janssen 54). On the other hand, the people of Ende, on the southern coast of Flores Island (now East Nusa Tenggara), among the Lesser Sunda Islands near Timor, also encounter errant currents due to "a storm and the luck of typhoon winds" (*temporal e fortuna de ventos Tuphon*, Mills 67; Janssen 55) to land on this new continent of gold. This event is again authenticated with a certificate, requested by Erédia, which gives the account by Pedro de Carvalhaes, captain of the Portuguese fort in Ende (Mills 69; Janssen 56–57). These narratives of discoveries suggest that a chance storm can close the distance between known and unknown. In fact, Australian contact with the Makassar peoples of South Sulawesi may well have predated European "discovery."[42]

Erédia says he intended to explore Luca Antara for himself but was detained in Melaka due to the attacks on the Portuguese fort from the joint forces of the Malay court exiled in Johor and the Dutch. Instead, he claims service in building forts in Muar and elsewhere to defend the straits of Singapore and in enforcing Portuguese rule in the town of Kota Baru, captured in 1588. In the end, Erédia made discoveries only in the environs of Melaka: "And most of the time was spent in the discovery of the hinterlands [*sertão*] of Melaka, which was wholly seen, and reconnoitered by the said Manuel Godinho de Erédia, in the capacity of discoverer [*descobridor*] of which he made maps and chorographic descriptions [*plantas e discripsões chorographicas*]" (Mills 72; Janssen 58). Despite aspirations to find the new, he ends up mapping what was already known.

3.3 Autobiography As Travel Literature

If Erédia imbues his narratives of discovery with the waywardness of romance, his own autobiography is also defined by romance. The story of how his parents met is made of the stuff of Christian-Muslim intercultural romance with a long literary history stretching back to the Middle Ages. Erédia's habit of reading the present in light of ancient and biblical histories extends to an engagement with the genre of medieval romance. His self-identified *mestiço* origin makes him of particular interest to studies of hybridized go-betweens, but what has been overlooked is how his autobiography is also a travel narrative. Just as his accounts of accidental discoveries have at their heart native actors, a closer examination of Erédia's autobiography also reveals a native, his mother, at its core.

Erédia's brief autobiography, "Sumario da vida," is an appendix to *Tratado Ophirico*. As the title suggests, it is a life summary giving the outline of his career. The modern editors, Juan Gil and Rui Manuel Loureiro, note that it is "a typical 'letter of service'" (Gil and Loureiro 160n597). To establish his noble lineage, it starts with his parents' ancestry: his father's connection to a noble Aragonese family and his mother's identity as daughter of the King of Supa. We get the merest hint of the story of the bride abduction. His mother's baptism in Machoquique (Bacukiki) in South Sulawesi was performed, he says, at the request of the Makassar kings on his father Juan de Heredia's advice, but the latter then sailed to Melaka with Elena Vessiva, "his wife"

[42] Watercraft images documented on rock art in northwestern Arnhem Land, Northern Territory, Australia depict Makassan *praus*, of which the earliest dates to before 1664 CE and possibly even earlier in the 1500s (Taçon et al., "A Minimum Age"; May, "Painted Ships" 85).

(*sua companheira*, Mills 265; Gil and Loureiro 160). At the time, Elena was "possessor of the state of Bacukiki" (*propietaria do estado de Machoquique*, Mills Gil and Loureiro 160), but with her flight power devolved onto her parents. All this, Erédia hastens to add, is recorded in the Makassar historical chronicle, "Carraem Talot" (Mills 265; Gil and Loureiro 160), perhaps the *Talloq Chronicle*, thus establishing a dual chain of sources, Portuguese and native.

Erédia offers more details in chapter 25, "Concerning Christianity," in part I of the *Declaraçam*. Father Vicente Viegas was sent from Melaka on a mission to Bacukiki, where he built a church and converted the kings of Bacukiki and Supa. Erédia supplies, as he frequently does, a testimonial from Father Francisco Luis, the archdeacon and vicar-general of the Melakan see, in the form of a copy of archival records of the mission. While the "Sumario" speaks of Elena as Juan de Heredia's wife when they left South Sulawesi, the *Declaraçam* introduces a little ambiguity: "When the time came for the junk to return to Melaka, at the moment of embarkation ... there occurred a disturbance and a riot in which weapons were displayed, because Dona Elena Vessiva had secretly embarked in the junk in the company of Juan de Eredia, to whom she was married [*estava casada*] or betrothed [*desposada*] against the wishes of her parents" (Mills 55–56; Janssen 43). In the "Sumario," Elena is an appendage of her husband; here, she has agency, stealing away out of love. Whether married or only betrothed, she chose Juan. Their union is publicly acknowledged in the church in Melaka where Elena took Juan "as her husband" (*recebeo por marido*, Mills 56; Janssen 43v).

The romance is thus a travel narrative. Juan's voyage with the mission out to South Sulawesi is repeated in a return voyage with a stowaway. Moreover, the marriage is a tale of adventure: while her relations gather on the beach with weapons in search of the Portuguese, the administrator gave command for an immediate departure to avoid trouble and deaths (Mills 56; Janssen 43). Elena's escape offends her relatives but their conversion is so authentic they remain Christians.

While Erédia presents both of his parents as heroic travelers – the phrase "rebolico de armas" (Janssen 43) suggests Juan was prepared to fight for his lady – it is his mother who takes the most action. Not only does she choose Juan, like the converting Muslim women of romance, Elena also later acts as a mediator. After twelve years, with a generational change of rulers when her cousin Tamolina is queen, she "wished to repair the breach of friendship and to restore the old-time intercourse and commerce" (Mills 56). Writing letters of reconciliation to the kings of Bacukiki and of Supa and Linda, she wishes to "recover that old communication and commerce" (*recuperar aquella antiga comonicação e comercio*) (Janssen 43v).

Letters (*cartas*) of course are key documents for Erédia, who literally strews his text with them. Elena effectively acts by writing: "by means of these letters she opened the gates of commerce and pacts [*comercio e tratto*] of the Portuguese with the Makassarese" (Janssen 43v; Mills 56). With a "noble ambassador" (*embaxador fidalgo*, Mills 56; Janssen 43v) as intermediary to carry her letters, she is placed in the position of a royal master, and an effective one in reviving trade. In gratitude, the Sulawesi kings send presents until her dying day. A native woman becomes traveler and adventurer, settler in a new country, mediator and ambassador.

3.4 Conclusion

Like Pires, Erédia sees Portuguese destiny as Solomonic and considers the Portuguese successors to the Malays. Focusing on the fort in his chorographical description of Melaka, he emphasizes the city's re-spatialization into a Portuguese one. In his racialization, he represents the more distant, putatively "wild" Banuas of the hinterland in ways more identifiably European, though linked to antiquity, namely the prophetic Sibyls, and transforms the local legend of the princes of Mount Ledang into familiar European frameworks.

However, the idea of discovery as the ascertaining of what has already been known, so suited to Pires's purposes in making the case for investment in Melaka, is in tension with an interest in newness. For Erédia, newness comes suddenly, unexpectedly, and randomly when ships go astray. Errant voyagers are not only European but also native. In particular, when read as a travel narrative, his autobiography reveals a celebrated traveler who is a native woman. Erédia hints at what would be explicit in Malay texts with non-European heroic travelers. My next section considers the native traveler in a Malay chronicle. Although the context is Islamic, travel is also framed in religious and prophetic terms.

4 Malay Travel in the Indian Ocean

Based on *Sejarah Melayu*, with whole episodes lifted from it, *Hikayat Hang Tuah* is a romance wrought out of chronicle history, possibly linked to the sultanate of Johor, successor to Melaka.[43] The protagonist, Hang Tuah, is the legendary *laksamana* or admiral of Melaka whose embassies to India, China, and the Middle East constitute embedded travel narratives in the text. However, scholarly

[43] Parnickle suggests that the text glorifies the admiral (*laksamana*) of Johor, Abd al-Jamil ("Epic Hero") while Braginsky views the work as reflecting the war between Johor and the Sumatran kingdom of Jambi in the 1650s and 1680s ("*Hikayat Hang Tuah*"; *Turkic-Turkish Theme*, 53–61). The work is also indebted to *Sejarah Melayu*.

commentary often broaches travel only obliquely. The overemphasis on the work as "legendary romance [*legandarische Roman*]" or "national heroic-historic epic" overlooks the work's character as travel literature (Hooykaas, *Over Maleise literatuur* 75–76; Braginsky, *Turkic-Turkish Theme* 53).[44]

Hikayat Hang Tuah's embedded travel narratives constitute an important subset of travel literature, whether European, Indo-Persian, or Malay: the diplomatic account. The episode garnering the most interest is the Ottoman embassy, which, Vladimir Braginsky argues, is a contestatory "palimpsestic" borrowing from the history of Aceh, Johor's rival (Braginsky, *Turkic-Turkish* 54). I have previously considered the work's mercantilist appropriation of romance in Hang Tuah's figuration of the Islamic Alexander the Great (Ng, *Alexander* 303–32). Since Tuah performs the Hajj on his way to the Ottoman Empire, *Hikayat Hang Tuah* is also studied as a pilgrimage narrative. Eric Tagliacozzo singles it out as an inaugural Malay Hajj narrative, noting that it "gives more weight to the Hajj's importance in its worldview than any previous Malay text" (Tagliacozzo, *Longest Journey* 95).[45] Diplomatic travel is intertwined with pilgrimage.

Pilgrimage routes were also conduits for literary transmission. Mapping an Arabic cosmopolis linking South and Southeast Asia, Ronit Ricci argues, "Literary networks connected Muslims across boundaries of space and culture, and they helped introduce and sustain a complex web of prior texts and new interpretations that were crucial to the establishment of both local and global Islamic identities" (Ricci, *Islam Translated* 1–2). Unsurprisingly, Tuah takes the same route as Sultan Bahadur's envoy, discussed in the Introduction – a stop first in Jeddah, completing the Hajj in Mecca, before proceeding to Istanbul. His travels trace historical circuits in a long-standing maritime network.

Tuah's diplomatic journeys reveal the rivalrous emulation of mercantile societies. Journeys both to proximate and distant states involve the forging of new kinship relations, whether through royal marriage or adoption, by which strangers are incorporated into the new society. This is not touristic travel but rather travel as a permanent condition. Nor is it painful exile; this migration expands the horizon of opportunities. However, such relations are not without tension. Melaka's main regional rival is the Javanese kingdom of Majapahit. Equally a threat are the Portuguese, with whom Tuah comes into repeated conflict in his travels. These encounters at crucial Indian Ocean ports testify to the disruptive intersection of the discontinuous Portuguese empire with indigenous networks. Making sense of a world reordered by European arrival, the work represents early modern travel's transformation by armed warfare.

[44] Maier contests its widespread generic designation as national epic ("Epik That Never Was").

[45] *Hikayat Hang Tuah* is included in Hooker and Milner, *Perceptions of the Hajj*.

4.1 A Mobile Society

The focus on *Hikayat Hang Tuah*'s longest journey – the combined Hajj and Ottoman embassy – frames travel as an extraordinary condition rather than the mundane activity it was in island Southeast Asia. Its societies were extraordinarily mobile. An overview of travel in the region contextualizes the distant embassies, discussed next.

To begin with, Melaka's founding is a travel tale and the state a moveable city. The merchants of Bentan and Singapore, in the Riau Archipelago, invite the Malay king from the royal line of Palembang, Sumatra, to be their monarch. The kingdom's establishment is initiated by a sea voyage. Bentan's prosperity attracts new citizens like the protagonist's parents, who migrate to make a living.[46] The monarchy moves yet again when the king while hunting witnesses the auspicious event of a white mouse deer attacking his dogs, named Melaka after the tree found there (65). Many details of this *translatio res publicae* conform to *Sejarah Melayu*'s narrative.

Two patterns of mobility can be noted here. On the individual level, travel in search of employment is common. In his first adventure, an encounter with pirates, Tuah himself sets out to sea in his father's boat, described as "roaming [*merantau*] wherever possible to find income" (25). A term that means sailing along a coast or emigrating, in the latter sense *merantau* is a cultural tradition of Sumatra's Minangkabau, whose young men seek fortunes elsewhere (Murad, *Merantau*).

Mobility occurs also on the population level. Political power was not land-based. Anthony Reid explains, "The key to Southeast Asian social systems was the control of men. Land was assumed to be abundant, and not therefore an index to power . . . Society was held together by the vertical bonds of obligation between men" (Reid, "Introduction: Slavery" 8). This galactic polity finds power radiating from a royal center to the peripheries (Tambiah, "Galactic Polity").[47] Any loss of power prompts migration to new political centers, as in *Hikayat Hang Tuah*'s *translatio* from Bentan to Melaka, though deliberately planned.

Likewise, when the Portuguese attacked Melaka, the populace fled inland. Because Southeast Asian cities were unfortified, "siege warfare was a new experience"; Geoffrey Parker elaborates: "Since wars had previously been fought to secure slaves or tribute, rather than to annex more territory or acquire

[46] Citations given parenthetically from Kassim Ahmad's edition; translations are mine. For an English translation, see Muhammad Haji Salleh's version.

[47] Although criticized by Day and Reynolds, "Cosmologies" and Walker, *Legend*, among others, the broad argument holds.

new specific strategic bases, the best defence against attack was either immediate surrender (when the enemy appeared in overwhelming strength) or temporary flight (at all other times)" (Parker, *Military Revolution* 121–22). While the Portuguese built a stone fort to stay permanently, the Melakan court shifted to Johor. One episode involves repopulating a conquered country whose people had fled to the jungle (47).

Nor does *Hikayat Hang Tuah* make a strict distinction between settled and mobile peoples. While Portuguese sources treat Orang Laut (sea peoples), or *selates*, as belonging outside of settled civilization, *Hikayat Hang Tuah* shows them to be integral to Melaka's defensive force. Knowledgeable about the shoals and reefs of the Riau Archipelago, Orang Laut had a symbiotic relationship with Malay rulers as "guardians of the ruler's maritime trade lanes states" (L. Andaya, *Leaves* 177). Pires even records that they traditionally held the role of *laksamana* (235).[48] Aside from his role as *laksamana*, Tuah's mastery of the Riau seascape suggests a possible identity as Orang Laut, straddling the maritime-land boundary.

Travelers to Melaka range from temporary visitors to assimilating permanent residents. Two contrasting examples from *Hikayat Hang Tuah*'s early chapters outline the contexts of travel in the archipelago. The first is a Javanese noble, Patik Kerma Wijaya, forced into exile by the ill treatment of his king who kidnaps his daughter for a concubine, voyaging to seek service in Melaka. His travels trace regional circuits, first to the coastal Javanese kingdom of Tuban, then to Jayakerta – the port that would become Dutch Batavia and modern Jakarta – and thence sailing to Bentan before being received at the Melakan court. Rather than individual travel, he comes with seven thousand followers, who settle with him as immigrants. As a transplant, Kerma Wijaya is a valuable cultural mediator, sent as an ambassador (*rajaduta*, or king's messenger) on the marriage embassy to Majapahit due to his knowledge of Javanese laws (*perintah Jawa*, 110), where his hybridity is noted: "You are Malay, how is it that you behave like a Javanese? Who are you?" (117).

The second example, Raja Culan, prince of Ceylon (Sailan), hearing of Melaka's princess, decides to woo her (446). Traveling in style, his vessel is as large as a country, on which they plant coconuts and betel, reminiscent of the Ming treasure ships (448). Wishing to tour the archipelago, to Terengganu, on the Peninsula's east coast, and Patani, his travel is for pleasure: he wishes to play (*bermain*, 450), to see the country's views (*temasya negeri*, 450), and to participate in cockfighting (*sabungan*, 452).

As Clifford Geertz notes in his seminal work on cockfighting, the term *sabung* for cock, with the double entendre, has a range of metaphorical

[48] On Tuah as Orang Laut, see Ng, *Alexander* 312–15.

meanings from "hero" to "man of parts," from "bachelor" to "dandy" or "lady-killer" (Geertz, "Deep Play" 418). A prince on a marriage quest obsessed with cockfighting desires to prove his manly prowess against the prince of Terengganu. However, both princes end up losing when a supernatural cock sinks Culan's ship and burns the Terengganu palace. Culan's recklessness so angers Melaka's king that he sends Tuah to conquer Terengganu (455–58). The episode paints a critical picture of flaunting visitors.

As a traveler, the protagonist Tuah occupies both the position of visitor and of a permanent resident. Tuah joins the embassy to Majapahit as *panglima muda* (young commander) to provide security. While *Hikayat Hang Tuah*'s distant embassies attract the most attention as travel narrative, the first part too is concerned with ambassadorial travel, but travel is motivated by marriage diplomacy. Practiced globally among dynastic realms, marriage diplomacy was often used to constrain wars. Ironically, here marriage diplomacy brings out hostilities between Majapahit and Melaka. Later, due to backbiting at court, Tuah is exiled by his king. To regain trust, he journeys to Inderapura to win for his king the prime minister's daughter, Tun Teja. To do so, he gets himself adopted by her nursemaid. In Inderapura, when his hosts apologize for not being pure Malay, he downplays differences to fit in better, saying, "Melakans are hybrid (*kacukan*) Malays, mixed with the Majapahit Javanese" (189).

Travel is endemic in the text. A plethora of travelers trace well-worn circuits made mundane by familiarity. The first part's journeys reveal the Malay Archipelago's dense regional interconnections connecting Melaka to Jambi, Palembang, and Inderapura in Sumatra, to Pahang, and to Jayakarta and Majapahit in Java, as well as further afield to Siam (Thailand). Although more distant, India's numerous connections to the archipelago are evident in the exchange of embassies not just with Melaka but also with Majapahit. Ambassadorial gifts, such as the Portuguese and Chinese horses the Indian embassy offers Majapahit, demonstrate international trade links (122). Prince Culan's own journey is prompted by Melaka's king's act of sending representatives to Ceylon to buy gems (*permata intan*, 444). Distant embassies, discussed next, are extensions of regional networks, though they map out the major arteries of the Indian Ocean trade circuits.

4.2 City and Court

While European travel writing devotes space to descriptions and categorizations of peoples, Malay writing lacks this explicit "ethnographic impulse" (Rubiés, "Travel Writing and Ethnography" 242). In part, this stems from a contrary impulse to seeing foreign, especially trade, relations in kinship terms. I've previously argued that kinship relations structure political ties in *Hikayat Hang Tuah*: Tuah crosses cultural and political boundaries with ease by getting adopted into foreign societies (Ng, *Alexander* 321–27). Yet the text is not without an interest in the exotic. It incorporates place descriptions, focusing not on human difference but rather on the built environment, dwelling especially on the grandeur of the foreign city and court. A work of traditional literature, *Hikayat Hang Tuah*'s links to oral performance means that it exhibits such devices as episodic repetition. The ambassadorial journey is one such repeated motif. Within that motif are descriptions of the city and court as submotifs, though some details are changed to suit the location. These descriptions appear only in embassies to distant states and not in those to proximate ones such as Siam, drawing the boundary between the archipelago and beyond.

The first embassy to India sets the model for the embedded travelogue. Docking first at Nagapatam (Nagapatnam), Tuah travels to the interior to the court of Vijaya Nagaram. The capital of the Deccan Vijayanagara Empire, founded in 1336 and lasting until 1565 when defeated in the battle of Talikota – a successor state was reestablished at Penukonda until it finally collapsed from internal dissensions in the seventeenth century – it was a destination also visited and described by European travelers.[49] *Hikayat Hang Tuah* primarily gives attention to the fortified city's magnificent grandeur and its fine workmanship:

> After several days' journey the fortified city [*kota*] of Vijayanagar appeared covered like combed cotton. Upon approach the Admiral saw how the gates were wonderfully carved with figures of animals. They were said to be made of crystal with a layer of black stone like the shimmering of beetle wings; on one layer the Admiral saw that the story of Rama [from the *Ramayana*] was etched and on another the performance of the victorious Pandavas [the *Mahabharata* in Malay] and on yet another written the various types of forest animals and the door was forged of a copper alloy. There were thousands of temples in the county of magnificent workmanship and a thousand mosques where the *anjuvanttar* [clan of Muslim cloth-weavers] worship and thousands of tents of woven wool spread out where all the merchants trade and keep shop. (391)

The first simile used for the city – the comparison to combed cotton – alludes to the main export from India to Southeast Asia, cloth. Combed cotton is refined; with impurities removed, it is softer and stronger than regular cotton. The material construction of the fortified city itself projects both strength and beauty.

[49] See Portuguese travelogues by Domingo Paes, circa 1525, and Fernão Nunes, dated 1535, in *Chronica dos reis de Bisnaga*, ed. Lopes; for an English translation, see Sewell, *Forgotten Empire*. For a discussion, see Rubiés, *Travel* 223–50.

The gates are made of valuable stone that reflects light.[50] The carvings display cultural and biological knowledges, showing scenes from the great Indian epics – like the walls of Troy Aeneas encounters – and recording information on wildlife. The civilizational greatness of the city is marked in the numbers of its houses of worship, catering to Hindus and Muslims. Finally, the city's commercial strength lies in the numbers of merchants, counted by the tents where they trade their wares.

That Vijayanagar is the first location described is in keeping with its historical importance. Before 1570, it was one of three major urban centers in South India, with a population of between three hundred thousand and four hundred thousand (Subrahmanyan, *Political Economy* 22–23). In comparison, London in 1500 had a population of only fifty thousand. The Malay word for city, *kota*, which can mean fort, comes from Sanskrit and has family resemblances with terms for fort from South Indian vernaculars: *kōṭṭai* (Tamil), *kōṭe* (Kannada), and *kōṭa* (Telegu).

Despite the apparent formulaic character of *Hikayat Hang Tuah*'s description, it is part of a widely shared "historical imagination of India … in … Western and Eastern narratives about a fabled land both rich and powerful" (Deshpande, "The Indian Fort" 127). The fort's description is central to this imagination. As Anirudh Deshpande shows, the organization of political states in India around fortified cities, which concentrated military and fiscal powers, has a long indigenous history. Despite the association of forts with modern European colonization, Europeans only imported some new methods of construction. *Hikayat Hang Tuah*'s descriptions of fortified cities encountered in the embassies assert an Asian mercantile and political system that rivals, if not overshadows the text's one European fort: the Portuguese fort in Melaka. Given Portuguese transformation of Melaka into a European fortified city, the paean to Vijayanagar – and to other Asian imperial cities – is, I argue, contestatory, especially, as I will show, when set against Tuah's repeated encounters with hostile Portuguese in these same spaces.

Vijayanagar's prestige redounds on the king of Melaka as his ally and Tuah is given a warm reception. The second set of descriptions in the embedded travelogues is of the court when Tuah meets the king, Kisna Rayan, a representation of the historical Krisynadevaraya (r. 1508–30):

> At that time Kisna Rayan had appeared attended by all the kings and princes and prime ministers, eunuchs, heralds and guards all. His majesty sat on

[50] Domingo Paes notes high hills leading into the city that were called gates (*portas*), but also records "city gates" and an outer "gate with a wall that encloses all the other enclosures of the city," made "of massive stonework" with citadels and a moat (Sewell, *Forgotten Empire* 242, 253).

> a golden throne studded with precious gems fringed with pearls. Next five hundred crowned kings sat in attendance to the right of Kisna Rayan while five hundred other crowned kings sat to his left. Seventy thousand helmeted knights in chain mail stood to his right and seventy thousand knights to his left, complete with their armor and weapons. A thousand war elephants stood to Kisna Rayan's right, all caparisoned with chain mail, and seven thousand war horses stood to his [left]. (392)

The description of court is similarly monumental, with the king's majesty measured in the number of his attendants. Although formulaic, this representation of courtly splendor by the sheer numbers of attendants and courtiers is not unlike those of European travel writing. Compare Thomas Dallam's (1575–1630?) account of the Ottoman court:

> I stood dazzling my eyes with looking upon his [the Grand Seignior's] people that stood behind him, which was four hundred persons in number. Two hundred of them were his principal pages ... They were appareled in rich cloth of gold made in gowns to the midleg ... The third hundred were dumb men, that could neither hear nor speak, and they were likewise in gowns of rich cloth of gold and Cordovan buskins; ... The fourth hundred were all dwarfs, ... and they were all appareled in gowns of cloth of gold. (Dallam, *Diary* 69–70)

In *Hikayat Hang Tuah*, the Vijayanagara king is attended not just by ministers, eunuchs, and heralds, but also by kings and princes to suggest the imperial might that subdued so many princedoms into tributaries. The king's military strength is highlighted, with special attention given to animals used for war, the elephants and horses that are royal symbols and that constitute important trade among Indian Ocean courts. Melaka's king even sends an embassy to Siam specifically to purchase elephants.

A second description of the king, visiting the coastal trading port, similarly emphasizes his enormous entourage. This description underscores his military capacity, for also in attendance are *kesateria* (kshatriya, the second-highest social caste, comprising the warrior aristocracy) and *pendekar* (swordsmen), all armed (395). Notably, among them are seventy thousand Portuguese subjects (*rakyatnya Feringgi tujuh puluh ribu*), Malabarese, people from Calicut, and Hindis (*Malabari dan Kalikut dan Hindi*), also armed, demonstrating the court's cosmopolitanism (395).

The pattern of paired descriptions of city and court is replicated in the embassies to China and the Ottoman Empire. The embassy to China is dispatched not by the king of Melaka but by the king of India. Using foreign visitors as ambassadors was not unheard of: the Safavid Shah Abbas (r. 1588–1629) employed the English Sherley brothers, Anthony and Robert, as his ambassadors to Europe. Such a mission honors Tuah's diplomatic skills.

China's description highlights its wealth: "The Admiral saw that the craftsmanship of the county was of wonderful manufacture; its seven-layered city made of white stone and the gate from copper alloy. Then the Admiral saw that the country had thousands of alleys and streets, all sheathed in white stone like combed cotton" (411). The repeated simile of combed cotton (*kapas sudah terbusar*) is now applied to pavement stones. The focus is on Chinese urban density and their craftsmanship. "There are so many strange crafts that we have never seen, because the people of this country of China are ingenious [*banyak hikmatnya*]" (411).

For the Chinese court, the description dwells on emperor's rich throne shaped like a dragon (*naga*), though he is also protected by armed guards (413). Touring the country, Tuah sees "several hundred houses of worship, of marvelous manufacture and painted with various figures of animals as though they were alive" (414). One statue as large as a hill is heard crying, due to human wickedness, with a voice like thunder, and below the statue "thousands were catching its tears, both men and women" (414), for the tears purportedly cleanse one's sin. The experience is unusual: Tuah is "seeing what he had never seen before" (414).

The embassy to the Ottomans – called Benua Rom, land of the Romans (491) – is farthest and most elaborate, befitting their political importance as Muslim allies. The goal is military: to purchase cannon (*bedil meriam*). Because his heir, Princess Mount Ledang (*Puteri Gunung Ledang*, 490), is female, the king plans to fortify Melaka with cannon (*kotai dengan bedillah negeri Melaka ini*, 490) to establish a permanent peace. The word *kota*, used for the fortified city of Vijayanagar, is turned into a verb. Melaka will transform into Vijayanagar, or perhaps, given the work's dating, it alludes to the fortifications the Portuguese added.

Puteri Gunung Ledang's story departs from *Sejarah Melayu*, where she is an enchantress whom Melaka's king woos unsuccessfully. Here she is repurposed into a weak female ruler to explain Melaka's fall. Further signs of Melaka's weakness are revealed in the mission's problems, all the more important due to Ottoman greatness: "the king of Rome is a great king and a protector of religion" (*Raja Rom itu raja besar lagi wali Allah*, 491).[51] With suzerainty over the holy cities of Arabia after their conquest of the Mamluks in 1517, the emperor's spiritual gifts come from his role as protector of the holy shrines. The difficulty comes not only from the distance but also from the dangers:

[51] The Arabic term *wali Allah*, which literally means "friend of God," is used to indicate a saint or one marked by divine favor.

"The country of Rome is exceedingly distant sailing and it is said that there are many enemies (*permusuhan*) on the way" (491), including the Portuguese.

The Ottoman episode departs in signal ways from previous embassies. Diplomatic relations with India and China are part of *Sejarah Melayu*, but this episode has no analog there. Rather, it alludes to the historical missions sent by Aceh during the reign of Alauddin Riayat Syah Al-Kahar (r. ca. 1539–71) to the courts of Suleiman the Magnificent (r. 1520–66) and Selim II (r. 1566–74) to obtain military assistance, including purchase of large cannons, against the Portuguese. Vladimir Braginsky argues that *Hikayat Hang Tuah*'s Turkish episode appropriates a similar one from Acehnese works such as *Bustan al-Salatin* (*Garden of Kings*) and *Hikayat Aceh* to valorize Melaka (standing in for Johor) (Braginsky, "Co-opting"). The embassy to Istanbul (*Rom*) is intertwined with the Hajj pilgrimage, like Bahadur's mission, and a stop in Egypt, preludes that underline Ottoman prestige. It is both a *riḥla sifariyya*, an account of an embassy, and a *riḥla hijaziyya*, a narrative of a Hajj, suggesting the continuing influence of religious pilgrimage as a structuring device for early modern travel and its narratives.

For this embassy, Tuah traces a more complicated route, starting where most Southeast Asian pilgrims would: the port of Aceh, known in the Malay world as Serambi Mekkah, the verandah of Mecca, the embarkation point for pilgrims. Next is Pulau Dewa, or Dewa Island, referring to Sri Lanka. After that they arrive in Mocha, a Yemeni port by the horn of Africa. Tuah is informed that Mocha lies to the right but to the left is the land of Habsyah, the Arabic name for Ethiopia (494).

From Mocha they sail to Jeddah, the port city on the Red Sea and gateway to Mecca. But before traveling overland to Mecca, Tuah makes a stop in Jeddah to visit the Tomb of Eve (*Siti Hawa*, 494). This episode follows the general outlines of the Indian embassy, with Tuah receiving a warm reception from the *syahbandar* at the port city due to his linguistic facility as well as from the ruler, titled *Malek*, from the Arabic for king. Tuah undergoes a double adoption here, received in kinship affinity by the *syahbandar* and by the Malek: they use familial terms of address, calling Tuah son (*anakku*), and themselves father (*ayahanda*, 495, 497). With the month of the Hajj nearing, Tuah's company joins the Malek's caravan to journey overland to Mecca, after which they visit Medina.

The Hajj differs from the embassies in its religious focus rather than on built architecture and courtly grandeur. Although the Melakans are impressed by the country's wealth, witnessing the large gifts of gold and silver brought by the Egyptians and Syrians – they are "astonished (*hairanlah*) to see the wealth and greatness of the Arabs" (499) – the narrative focuses on rituals pilgrims normally perform and as such forms a brief travel guide to the Hajj: stoning of the devil (رمي الجمرات, throwing of the place of pebbles), involving throwing pebbles at three pillars called *jamarāt* – in *Hikayat Hang Tuah* they are named “Jamratul Akabah, Jamratul Wusta and Jamratul Ula”; prayers at the Ka‘aba; and drinking from the Zamzam well (500). But they also take the opportunity to sightsee. In Mecca, they “visited all the graves of syeikhs and saints (*wali Allah*), prophets; they did all the places for visitation (*ziarah*)” (499); they do the same in Medina, visiting the graves of holy and important personages from Islamic history (500). *Ziarah* has the specific meaning of going on pilgrimage or visiting holy sites though it can mean, more generally, simply touring. Tuah’s tour continues in Egypt, which, like the holy cities, is under Ottoman suzerainty.

Mixing religious duty with secular endeavors, Tuah visits the grave of the prophet Joseph (*Nabi Allah Yusuf*, 501) but also meets the ruler, Ibrahim Kakan, whom he impresses by speaking the “Roman language” (*bahasa Rom*, 509) – that is, Ottoman Turkish. Narratively, the visit to Egypt functions as a prelude to the Ottoman court by including a description of Istanbul in a secondhand narration: Tuah and his companion are “astonished to hear Ibrahim Kakan’s relations” (511). Ottoman magnificence is part of the circulation of news. A well-known place, Istanbul is a destination in the way that Tomé Pires frames Melaka.

Considerably longer and more elaborate than any previous geographical description, Ibrahim’s account begins with the immensity of fortified Istanbul: it has “seven layers (*lapis*) and moats and six large gates. Entering by the gate where the sun rises it takes three months to walk to the gate where the sun sets; the distance between the gate to the interior and the gate to the shore is just as far. It takes twelve months to traverse the country’s perimeter” (510). The city walls and gates are made of beautiful stone and metal. The description extends to the surrounding country, from the immense lake in the middle of the country with an island where the sultan keeps a garden (*bustan*, 511), stocked with wild animals for his hunt and planted with all kinds of flowers and fruits, to the seashore with a “magic dragon” (*naga hikmat*, 512), from whose mouth water flows.

While the focus is the natural environment, nature is both artful and shaped by art. The river, adorned with polished stone, is where the sultan fishes under the shade of a spreading tree like a green umbrella (511). The gardens have pergolas shaped like dragons, with multiple ponds or bathing pools, bridges, and islands. Some structures are identified by the makers’ ethnic identity: the decorated warehouse fronted with a hall for royal feasting, adorned with gold and silver banana trees, is of Turkish manufacture (*perbuatan orang Benua Turki*, 513); another hall, decorated with scenes of gamekeepers with elephants hunting lions and flying birds, and pillars carved with coiling dragons and pouncing tigers, is made by the Chinese (*perbuatan orang Cina*, 514). One garden combines an impossible variety of temperate and tropical fruit: apples, grapes, and pomegranates intermingle with Southeast Asian mangosteen, rambutan, langsat, nangka (jackfruit), durian, and "buah Melaka," the fruit of the Melaka tree (Indian gooseberry tree or *Phyllanthus emblica*). Meant to impress Southeast Asian readers, some elements, from Chinese decorations to local fruits, also make the foreign space familiar.

At the Ottoman court, the narrative begins like the embassy to India, with a description of the fortified city that largely repeats the reported version. Wonder goes the other way as well. The embassy's reception elicits amazement among the "Romans" (*orang Rom*, 522), and the sultan swiftly grants Melaka's request for armaments. Braginsky reads the text as Johor's political response to Aceh in a literary war by depicting the Melakans as more successful in obtaining Ottoman military aid.

Yet the embassy is not without roadblocks. After having been sometime in Istanbul, "tried as he could to see the king of Rome he [Tuah] was unsuccessful. Not only could he not see the king, he could not even get a glimpse of the throne" (524). He approaches the ministers for a royal audience by giving his credentials of having led embassies to India, China, Majapahit, Siam, and Brunei, as well as to Mecca and Medina. Further he notes embassies not recounted in the text: to Ethiopia (negeri Habsyah), Portugal (negeri Feringgi), and the Low Countries (negeri Wolanda), where they could "all have audience with and speak with their king" (524).

Tuah's travels map both regional and global circuits, and like Sultan's Bahadur's dream from Garcia da Orta's anecdote, combine long-standing Indian Ocean circuits with new ones introduced by the Europeans. But the Indian Ocean saw increasing intrusion by the Europeans, especially the Portuguese.

4.3 Portuguese Disruptions

Tuah's ambassadorial travels map Southeast Asia's trade links stretching from the Ottoman Empire to China. But they are marked by repeated encounters with belligerent Portuguese. As Tuah traces increasingly wider circuits, the conflicts intensify into open warfare and the Portuguese eventually attack Melaka. His travels affirm Southeast Asia's deep connections with trading partners to the East and West, but the repeated confrontations depict Portuguese disruption of maritime routes. The Portuguese transformed Indian Ocean travel, turning trade and pilgrimage routes into zones of conflict and re-spatializing port cities such as Melaka into European settlements.

Melakans' conflict with the Portuguese is depicted in three acts, each encounter more intense than the previous. But report of their hostilities precedes these episodes. Significantly, the report comes in an exchange between two ships belonging to the great Indian merchant Parmadewan, one sailing from Melaka, the other returning from China. The captain of the China ship reports encountering seven Portuguese galleons (*ghali*, 98) firing at them; firing back, they sank one but others got away.[52] The captain predicts that the six galleons will attack the bay of India in revenge. Indeed, the Melaka ship – on a diplomatic mission from a royal prince back to the king of India – soon runs into a fleet of thirteen, which the ship's climber (*jurutinggi*) spots as an "armada" (99). In the skirmish, they easily defeat the Portuguese by first destroying their high mast and next by firing at their oars until "the captain of the galleon raised the white pennant as a sign of surrender" (99). That the exchange happens between Indian trading ships plying the route between India and China highlights Portuguese encroachment on preexisting trade routes. The Indians' treatment of the Portuguese after their victory – they invite the Portuguese captain for an audience with Parmadewan – suggests an initial attempt at incorporating these newcomers.

These contretemps reflect a historical truth. The Portuguese made their presence felt, attacking key ports like Melaka and shipping. Portuguese militarization of the oceanic space was new to the region: "Before the arrival of the Portuguese in the Indian Ocean in 1498 there had been no organised attempt by any political power to control the sea-lanes and the long-distance trade of Asia" (Chaudhuri, *Trade* 14). Asians quickly adapted. Within the first two decades of Portuguese contact, western Indian coastal states turning increasingly to firearms, though European firearms did not confer the same advantage in Asia. Firearms came to India and beyond through the Middle East, with Deccan kings employing the services of Ottoman artillery men as well as Portuguese renegades to shape a hybrid tradition fusing European and Mamluk-Ottoman methods (Subrahmanyam and Parker, "Arms and the Asian").[53]

Ottoman influence spread to Southeast Asia; diplomatic exchanges with Aceh brought cannon and cannon-making technologies as well as military men to the region (Reid, "Sixteenth-Century Turkish"; Casale, *Ottoman Age*, chapter 5). Aceh's Sultan Iskandar Muda (r. 1607–36) even "maintained a palace guard composed of military slaves, similar to the Ottoman

[52] I translate the word *ghali* as galleon when referring to Portuguese vessels. The Malay word *ghali*, from the Portuguese *gale*, can refer to a native galley. On early modern Southeast Asian ship technology, see L. Andaya, "Interactions" 28–35.

[53] On firearms in Asia before European arrival, see Khan, *Gunpowder and Firearms*; for the hybrid tradition, see Daehnhardt, *Bewitched Gun*, and Eaton, "'Kiss my Foot,'" especially 310.

Janissaries, captured in war" and "received Abyssinian slave officers (next to Turkish soldiers) from the Porte" and his court was "reminiscent of a Middle-Eastern state" (Wink, *Al-Hind* 16). The Portuguese, however, spurred the building of fortifications: they built the *A Famosa* stone fort in Melaka and influenced the design of the Makassar fortress, of Sombaopu, erected around the royal palace and armed with heavy European guns (Subrahmanyam and Parker, "Arms and the Asian" 24–26).

Intriguingly, the battle strategy in *Hikayat Hang Tuah*'s episode is reminiscent of Portuguese naval tactics. Due to small numbers, the Portuguese avoided engaging in close fighting. King Manuel's instructions in February 1500 to commander Pedro Álvares Cabral, who bombarded Calicut, was "not to come to close quarter with them [hostile ships] if you can avoid it, but only with your artillery are you to compel them to strike sail . . . so that this war may be waged with greater safety, and so that less loss may result to the people of your ships" (Greenlee, *Voyage* 183, qtd. in Subrahmanyam and Parker, "Arms and the Asian" 19). Sanjay Subrahmanyam and Geoffrey Parker comment, "Portuguese fleets overseas normally deployed in line ahead and battered their enemies without board" while, as in a skirmish in 1502, "Indians, encouraged by their numerical superiority, closed for battle" (Subrahmanyam and Parker, "Arms and the Asian" 19). In *Hikayat Hang Tuah*, the Indians adopt Portuguese methods by firing at and destroying enemy ships rather than boarding to overwhelm the opponent by their greater numbers.

The representation of Malay naval warfare also highlights use of firearms. One naval battle against Majapahit shows Malay deployment of both the Portuguese strategy of destroying enemy ships from afar and a native interpretation of new technology to do so. Shooting at the leading ship carrying the Javanese admiral, Hang Tuah breaks the shrouds (*temberang*) – standing rigging supporting the mast – and then the helm (*kemudi*), incapacitating the vessel (229). Some of the Javanese want to "batter the [enemy's] junk and galley" (*langar jong dan ghali*) so as to be "quickly certain of their task" (229), suggesting the tactic of boarding enemy ships to engage in close combat. However, observing Tuah's shooting (*kelakuan ... memanah*), the admiral decides to retreat (*undur*, 229). Tuah improbably shoots nine hundred and ninety arrows simultaneously (*anak panahku yang sembilan ratus sembilan puluh*, 229). In another episode, the Portuguese use matchlock guns (*istinggar*, from the Portuguese word *espingarda*, 417). Encountering cannon-fire, Tuah again deploys his bow (*busar*, 426), damaging the enemy's mast and helm to force a retreat.

Tuah's weapon seems both traditional and novel. The volley of shots recalls multi-shot, wheel-lock guns. Notably, firearms may have been termed bows:

Iqtidar Alam Khan argues that the term *kaman-i r'ad* (کمان رعد, thunder-bow), referring to a missile throwing device, in fifteenth-century Persian texts from South India, Central Asia and Iran, was "possibly an artillery piece worked with gunpowder" (Khan, "Firearms" 438).[54] Tuah's unusual bow suggests a literary transmutation of such a firearm. However, in the great naval battle between the Melakans and the Portuguese near the end of the work, discussed later, Tuah defeats the Portuguese with the usual method of boarding the enemy ship and "running amuck" (*mengamok*, 485) with his men.

Tuah's encounters with the Portuguese reflect a new danger to travel. Direct conflict with the Portuguese begins with a series of embassies cum trading expeditions. Conflicts occur at the port city rather than at the royal court in the interior. With the contestation primarily over access to maritime trade routes, Portuguese activities focus on the coast. Each encounter follows a similar pattern. The Melakans are told to dock at the harbor designated for the Portuguese envoy, but the sight of local authorities honoring the Malay fleet at their jetty angers the Portuguese.

In each case, the bellicose Portuguese are termed *soldadu*, meaning soldier, a direct linguistic borrowing from the Portuguese language (*soldado*). By using a Portuguese term, the text suggests that aggressive militancy is their own chosen identity. The Malays, in contrast, identify themselves as traders (*dagang*). In India, they reply: "Why do you forbid us? We are also traders. No matter where we're told to dock, there we'll drop anchor" (388). Nonetheless, the Malays are no pushovers: "If you want to fight with us, whether it's one-on-one or a general combat we will fight; we will also fight ship-to-ship" (388–89). Boasting of their numbers, the Malays assert their prowess in the willingness to engage in a wide range of combat: individual duels, warfare, or naval battles.

The Portuguese encounter in China repeats the Indian incident with minor variations, emphasizing the Malays' trading credentials while also underlining their military preparations. The conflict intensifies as the Portuguese become more aggressive. The Portuguese threaten: "Hey Malay and Indian, don't you dock here close to the captain's galley [*ghali*]. Now he comes to fire cannons at all your ships" (409). This speech provokes laughter among the Malays, who disregard the warning to moor their ship by the Portuguese galley. The Portuguese *soldadu* grows angrier: "Malays and Indians are without manners. They seem as though they want to fight with us, because they think they are many" (409).

The Malays again remind the Portuguese that they are traders (*dagang*), docking where told to by the harbormaster (*syahbandar*, 409), framing the

[54] Khan, "Early Use" and *Gunpowder and Firearms*.

opposition in terms of war versus trade, soldiers versus merchants. Although the Malays are accompanied by Indians, for it is officially an Indian embassy, they view the enmity as primarily one between themselves and the Portuguese: "The Portuguese and Malays are enemies [*seteru*]" (409). However, Portuguese hostility is directed at both Malays and Indians, suggesting enmity toward Asian traders as a whole. By telling them to take their dispute to sea, the harbormaster maintains the port as a place for trade.

Conflict breaks out again at the completion of the Malay-Indian embassy, with the Portuguese as aggressor and the Chinese as arbiter. Upon his return, the Portuguese captain becomes angry when informed of the perceived insult of the Malay ship harboring by their galley. Moreover, Tuah's ambassadorial letter is conveyed to the king while the Portuguese letter has stalled at the ministerial level (416). Out of anger, the captain arms his cannons with shot and positions his ship for attack at Tuah's departure. The Chinese forbid fighting in the bay and instruct them to take the quarrel out to sea. News of the fight travel swiftly to the harbormaster and from him to the four ministers, who criticize the Portuguese: "The ministers were angry and say, 'Truly the Portuguese are without manners!' Thus with utmost anger, they say, 'We haven't even responded to their letter!'" (417). While the Portuguese accuse the Malays and Indians of lack of manners, they eventually are found unmannerly by the Chinese. A third party occupies the role of civilizational arbiter, whose negative judgment of Portuguese lack is underlined by the diplomatic failure of the unanswered letter. Depicted as more than an equal match, the Malays' apparent displacement of the Portuguese at trading ports in these episodes reverses Portuguese ejection of native traders in the period of the *Estado da Índia*'s expansion.

Portuguese disruptions also reshaped the experience of travel across the Indian Ocean for pilgrims. The Hajj was a major impetus of travel and pilgrims took passage on trading ships. Portuguese presence put both the spice trade and pilgrimage at risk: the Portuguese patrolled the Red Sea entrance to Mecca, they attacked Mamluk ships carrying spices and pilgrims from India, and they battled fleets like the one from Calicut in 1504–05 that included a ship with a cargo of alms of gold and silver to be sent to the sharifs of Mecca (Pearson, *Pious Passengers* 88–90).

Mahmood Kooria goes further in seeing religious motive. "Both the *Estado* officials and their Jesuit allies tried their best to interrupt the pilgrimage" (Kooria, "Killed the Pilgrims" 17). In his jihadi poem, *Fatḥ al-mubīn* (*Great Conquest*), Muḥammad al-Kālikūtī (d. 1616?) laments that the Portuguese "forbade ships to set sail for Mecca, and this was the worst of the calamity, . . . restricted vessels from sailing on the sea, especially the vessels of the greater and lesser pilgrimage"

(M Khan, "Indo-Portuguese" 172, 176, stanzas 90 and 278). His brother, Zayn al-Dīn II (d. 1581?), author of the well-known *Tuhfat al-mujāhidīn* (*Gift to the Warriors of Faith*), also described Portuguese harassment of pilgrims:

> The Portuguese scoffed at the Muslims and held them up to scorn ... obstructed their journeys especially ḥajj journeys; ... set fire to their houses and mosques; trampled under feet and burned the Holy Qur'an and other religious books ... [They] killed the ḥajj pilgrims and persecuted them with all kinds of cruelties; captured them and kept them bound in heavy chains ... dragging them around in the streets and markets to sell them as slaves. (Zayn, *Tuḥfat* 56–57)

Portuguese attacks aimed at the Indian Ocean's economic and religious life.

The Hajj is a key element of Hang Tuah's travels. On his way to the Ottoman Empire, Hang Tuah stops in Jeddah to travel overland to Mecca. Early modern Hajj pilgrims also visited shrines and tombs of notable figures, visitations known as *ziyarah*: traveling to and from India in the 1550s, the Ottoman navigator Seydi Ali Reis (1498–1563) stopped at many sites.[55] Likewise, Tuah visits other shrines, namely the graves of Eve (*Siti Hawa,* 494, 498) and Joseph (*Yusuf*, 502), and he stops at the Nile because its headstream is said to originate in paradise (*syurga*, 501). Like Bahadur's mission, the Melakan embassy combines pilgrimage with a diplomatic visit to the Ottoman Empire whose purpose is both commercial and military as they intend to purchase large cannons (*bedil meriam*, 495) for which the Ottomans were famed. Such journeys thus had multiple and mutually reinforcing objectives.

However, departing from the pattern, Tuah does not encounter the Portuguese in the Middle East. Instead, the extended Ottoman episode, recounted over two chapters, 25 and 26, is framed by the Portuguese invasion of Melaka in chapters 24 and 28, with chapter 27 focusing on internal decline. The conclusion puts long-distance travel for trade and diplomacy in the context of Portuguese expansion. Melaka's invasion is triggered by the naval encounter off the Chinese coast, reported by the Portuguese captains, Dong [Dom] Manila and Dong Cuala, to their governor in Manila, who sails to Portugal to inform the king. Conflating Spain and Portugal, under Spanish rule between 1580 and 1640, the narrative traces, through the sequence of travel and the names given the captains, broad outlines of the Iberian maritime network. This network connects Europe with the East Indies – Manila was the administrative center of the Spanish East Indies since 1565 – and with the West, as Cuala may reference Xuala, the Spanish name for the Cheraw or Saraw tribe of North Carolina.

[55] See Sidi Ali Reis, *Travels* 23, 5–7, 8, 9, 32, 35, and *passim*; qtd. in Pearson, *Pious Passengers* 37–38, 59n5.

Melaka's fate is to be forcibly incorporated into the Iberians' global network. The Portuguese transform Melaka into a walled city: they "made a fort [*kota*]of black stones around the hill. Then they daubed it with chalk (*kapur*) that glittered with light, which appeared like combed cotton" (547). The language is similar to that for Asian fortified cities in Tuah's embassies, though much truncated. However, its construction from black stones is foregrounded and the color scheme is stark: the exterior white of the chalk hides a black interior, perhaps suggestive of a new European Black-and-white racialization.[56] This fort is a double of the Portuguese factory, itself associated with Portuguese perfidy, coming for trade but staying as invaders. In a version of the tale of the oxhide purchase, as with Dido's founding of Carthage, the Portuguese ask for land as wide as a piece of oxhide, but tear it to make ropes to claim a much larger space in front of Melaka's main gates: "they made a very large factory of great height, a very strong factory, with seven layers of embrasure for cannon" (544).[57] Their factory becomes a defensive fort when the Portuguese secretly bring in cannon in the dead of night to attack the city. Blame is put on the female monarch for refusing to listen to her ministers' warnings and to the lure of trade goods described as "wonderful" (*terlalu indah-indah*, 545).

Yet the narrative also resists Portuguese re-spatialization, as it ends with the retaking of Melaka in collaboration with the Dutch (*orang Wolanda*, 547). By ending with this episode from 1641, the narrative celebrates Johor's military action. Although the city is given to the Dutch, their rule does not extend to the surrounding country: "Because of the promise, the Dutch who reside in Melaka and Jayakarta (Batavia) did not take the country with all its rivers, even till today, and the story of Melaka is never mentioned but that it was ruled by the Johor people and the Dutch" (548). Portuguese re-spatialization is recuperated with a later, though partial, victory, where the country returns to Malay rule.

4.4 Conclusion

Like Pires and Erédia, *Hikayat Hang Tuah* frames travel in religious terms, not only in its depiction of the Hajj but also in the way travel is intertwined with conflict with Portuguese Christians. At the same time, the Portuguese had a deep impact on travel. Borrowed words such as *soldadu* and *istinggar* suggest how Portuguese became a sign of cosmopolitanism. Portuguese objects, such as the horse brought by the Indian embassy, entered international trade exchanges. Portuguese subjects added to the luster of Asian courts, as in the seventy thousand Portuguese at the Vijayanagara court (395). Portugal becomes a node in the diplomatic network. To gain audience with the Ottoman sultan,

[56] See Ng, "Making Race." [57] See Ng, *Alexander* 330–31.

Tuah boasts of welcome elsewhere, including in Portugal and the Low Countries (*negeri Feringgi dan negeri Wolanda*, 524), where all could approach the king. Most intriguing is the protagonist's use of the Portuguese language. While Tuah demonstrates fluency in the local languages in the embassies, he uses Portuguese not as a lingua franca, but, remarkably, as a secret language. In Tuban, Java, he speaks in Portuguese (*bahasa Feringgi*, 141) to warn his compatriots of the tricks of Majapahit's prime minister. In a diplomatic meeting with Inderapura, Tuah consults with his second-in-command in Portuguese so as not to be understood by the Inderapuran ministers (472).

Hikayat Hang Tuah thus depicts travel in a transitional period. Traders still plied the centuries-old spice routes and pilgrims trace the same routes to Mecca to perform the customary rituals. But the rhythms of travel were increasingly disrupted by Portuguese incursions. The re-spatialization of port cities like Melaka – depicted by both Pires and Erédia – were also accompanied by a linguistic transformation as Portuguese became more familiar. Just as the Portuguese turned to native texts to incorporate into their epistemologies, the Malays incorporated foreign objects, peoples, and knowledges. In its embedded travel narratives, *Hikayat Hang Tuah* fits Malays into a global system, even if it is one that must now also accommodate Europeans.

Bibliography

Primary

Barbosa, Duarte. *The Book of Duarte Barbosa: An Account of the Countries Bordering on the Indian Ocean and Their Inhabitants*. Ed. and trans. Mansel Longworth Dames. 2 vols. London: Hakluyt Society, 1918, 1921.

Ibn Battuta. *Voyages d'Ibn Batoutah: Texte Arabe, accompagné d'une traduction*. Ed. and trans. Charles Defrémery and Beniamino Raffaello Sanguinetti. 4 vols. Rpt. ed. Cambridge: Cambridge University Press, 1858, 2012.

Bowrey, Thomas. *A Geographical Account of Countries round the Bay of Bengal*. Ed. Sir Richard Carnac Temple. Cambridge: Hakluyt Society, 1905.

Chronica dos reis de Bisnaga. Ed. David Lopes. Lisbon: Impresa Nacional, 1897.

Coutre, Jacques de. *The Memoirs and Memorials of Jacques de Coutre: Security, Trade and Society in 16th- and 17th-Century Southeast Asia*. Ed. Peter Borschberg. Trans. Roopanjali Roy. Singapore: National University of Singapore Press, 2014.

Dallam, Thomas. *Diary*. In *Early Voyages and Travels in the Levant: I. The Diary of Master Thomas Dallam, 1599–1600. II. Extracts from the Diaries of Dr. John Covel, 1670–1670*. Ed. J. Theodore Bent. New York: Burt Franklin, 1893, 1–98.

Documentação Ultramarina Portuguesa. Ed. António da Silva Rego. 3 vols. Lisbon: Centro de Estudos Históricos Ultramarinos, 1960–63.

Erédia, Manuel Godinho de. "Eredia's Description of Malaca, Meridional India, and Cathay." Trans. John Vivian Gottlieb Mills. *Journal of the Malayan Branch of the Royal Asiatic Society* Vol. 9, Part 1, No. 109 (1930): 1–288.

Malaca L'Inde Méridionale et le Cathay: Manuscrit original autographe de Godinho de Eredia appurtenant a la Bibliothéque Royale de Bruxelles. Trans. Léon Janssen. Preface Charles Ruelens. Brussels: Librarie Européenne C. Muqardt, 1882.

Ordenações da Índia do Senhor Rei D. Manoel de Eterna Memoria, Informação verdadeira da Aurea Chersoneso, feita pelo antigo Cosmographo Indiano, Manoel Godinho de Eredia. Ed. Antonio Lourenço Caminha. Lisbon: Impressão Régia, 1807.

Suma de ávores e plantas da Índia Intra Ganges. Ed. John G. Everaert, J. Eduardo Mendes Ferrão, and Maria Cândida Liberato. Lisbon: Comissão Nacional para as Comemorações dos Descobrimentos Portugueses, 2001.

Tratado Ophirico, 1616. Ed. Juan Gil and Rui Manuel Loureiro. Lisbon: Centro Científico e Cultural de Macau, 2016.

Gama, Vasco da. *Em nome de Deus: The Journal of the First Voyage of Vasco da Gama to India, 1497–1499*. Trans. and ed. Glenn J. Ames. Leiden: Brill, 2009.

Greenlee, William B., ed. *The Voyage of Pedro Álvares Cabral to Brazil and India*. London: Hakluyt Society, 1938.

Haafner, Jacob. *Lotgevallen en vroegere zeereizen van Jacob Haafner*. Ed. C. M. Haafner. Amsterdam: Johannes van der Hey, 1820.

Hikayat Aceh. Ed. and intro. Teuku Iskandar. Kuala Lumpur: Yayasan Karyawan, 2001.

Hikayat Hang Tuah. Ed. Kassim Ahmad. Intro. Noriah Mohamed. Kuala Lumpur: Yayasan Karyawan/Dewan Bahasa dan Pustaka, 1964, rev. 1975, 1997.

Hikayat Hang Tuah: The Epic of Hang Tuah. Trans. Muhammad Haji Salleh. Ed. Rosemary Robson. Kuala Lumpur: Institut Terjemahan Negara Malaysia, 2010.

Mundy, Peter. *The Travels of Peter Mundy, in Europe and Asia, 1608–1667*. Vol. 3, Part 1. Ed. Sir Richard Carnac Temple. London: Hakluyt Society, 1919.

Orta, Garcia da. *Colloquies on the Simples and Drugs of India*. Trans. Sir Clements Markham. London: Henry Sotheran, 1913.

Colóquios dos simples e drogas he cousas medicinais da Índia. Goa, 1563.

Pires, Tomé. *Suma oriental*. Ed. Rui Manuel Loureiro. Lisbon: Centro Científico e Cultural de Macau, 2017.

The Suma oriental *of Tomé Pires: An Account of the East, from the Red Sea to China, Written in Malacca and India in 1512–1515*. Ed. Armando Cortesão. 2 vols. London: Hakluyt Society, 1944.

Purchas, Samuel. *Hakluytus Posthumus, or Purchas His Pilgrimes*. London, 1625.

Rijaluddin, Ahmad. *Ahmad Rijaluddin's Hikayat Perintah Negeri Benggala*. Ed. and trans. Cyril Skinner. The Hague: Martinus Nijhoff, 1982.

Sejarah Melayu: The Malay Annals. Ed. Cheah Boon Kheng. Transliteration by Abdul Rahman Haji Ismail. Kuala Lumpur: Malaysian Branch of the Royal Asiatic Society, 1998.

Sidi Ali Reis. *The Travels and Adventures of the Turkish Admiral Sidi Ali Reis in India, Afghanistan, Central Asia and Persia during the Years 1553–1556*. Trans. A. Vambéry. London: Luzac & Co., 1899.

Zayn al-Dīn al-Malībārī. *Shaykh Zainuddin Makhdum's Tuḥfat al-Mujāhidīn: A Historical Epic of the Sixteenth Century*. Trans. S. Muhammad Husayn Nainar. Kuala Lumpur: Islamic Book Trust; Calicut: Other Books, 2006.

Secondary

Alam, Muzaffar, and Sanjay Subrahmanyam. *Indo-Persian Travels in the Age of Discoveries, 1400–1800*. Cambridge: Cambridge University Press, 2007.

"A View from Mecca: Notes on Gujarat, the Red Sea, and the Ottomans, 1517–39/923–946 H." *Modern Asian Studies* Vol. 51, No. 2 (2017): 268–318.

Alegria, Maria Fernanda, Suzanne Daveau, João Carlos Garcia, and Francesc Relaño. "Portuguese Cartography in the Renaissance." In *The History of Cartography, Vol 3: Cartography in the European Renaissance*. Part 1. Ed. David Woodward. Chicago, IL: University of Chicago Press, 2007, 975–1068.

Andaya, Barbara Watson. "Cash Cropping and Upstream-Downstream Tensions: The Case of Jambi in the Seventeenth and Eighteenth Centuries." In *Southeast Asia in the Early Modern Era: Trade, Power, and Belief*. Ed. Anthony J. S. Reid. Ithaca, NY: Cornell University Press, 1993, 91–122.

"Imagination, Memory and History: Narrating India-Malay Intersections in the Early Modern Period." In *Narratives, Routes and Intersections in Pre-modern Asia*. Ed. Radhika Seshan. London: Routledge, 2017, 8–35.

"Upstreams and Downstreams in Early Modern Sumatra." *The Historian* Vol. 57, No. 3 (1995): 537–52.

Andaya, Barbara Watson, and Leonard Y. Andaya. *The History of Malaysia*. 2nd ed. Houndsmill: Palgrave Macmillan, 2001.

Andaya, Leonard Y. "Interactions with the Outside World and Adaptation in Southeast Asian Society, 1500–1800." In *The Cambridge History of Southeast Asia, Vol. 2: From c. 1500 to c. 1800*. Ed. Nicholas Tarling. Cambridge: Cambridge University Press, 1999, 1–57.

The Kingdom of Johor, 1641–1728. Kuala Lumpur: Oxford University Press, 1975.

Leaves of the Same Tree: Trade and Ethnicity in the Early Modern Period. Honolulu: University of Hawaii Press, 2008.

Aubin, Jean. "Duarte Galvão." In *Le latin et l'astrolabe: Recherche sur le Portugal de la renaissance, son expansion en Asie et les relations internationales*. 3 vols. Paris: Fondation Calouste Gulkenbian, 1996–2006, 1:11–48. Rpt. of *Arquivos do Centro Cultural Português* Vol. 9 (1975): 43–85.

"L'ambassade du Prêtre Jean à D. Manuel." *Mare Luso-Indicum* Vol. 3 (1976): 1–56.

Batchelor, Robert. "Crying a Muck: Collecting, Domesticity, and Anomie in Seventeenth-Century Banten and England." In *Collecting across*

Cultures: Material Exchanges in the Early Modern Atlantic World. Ed. Daniela Bleichmar and Peter C. Mancall. Philadelphia: University of Pennsylvania Press, 2011, 116–33.

Beckingham, C. F. "The Riḥla: Fact or Fiction?" In *Golden Roads: Migration, Pilgrimage and Travel in Medieval and Modern Islam.* Ed. Ian Richard Netton. Richmond, Surrey: Curzon Press, 1993, 86–94.

Berkwitz, Stephen C. *Buddhist Poetry and Colonialism: Alagiyavanna and the Portuguese in Sri Lanka.* Oxford: Oxford University Press, 2013.

Bethencourt, Francisco, and Diogo Ramada Curto, eds. *Portuguese Oceanic Expansion, 1400–1800.* Cambridge: Cambridge University Press, 2007.

Blackmore, Josiah. *Moorings: Portuguese Expansion and the Writing of Africa.* Minneapolis: University of Minnesota Press, 2009.

Borschberg, Peter. *Hugo Grotius, the Portuguese, and Free Trade in the East Indies.* Singapore: National University of Singapore Press, 2011.

"Three Early 17th-Century Maps by Manuel Godinho de Erédia." *Journal of the Malaysian Branch of the Royal Asiatic Society* Vol. 92, Part 2, No. 317 (2019): 1–28.

Boxer, Charles Ralph *The Portuguese Seaborne Empire, 1415–1825.* London: Hutchinson, 1969.

Braginsky, Vladimir. "Co-opting the Rival Ca(n)non: The Turkish Episode of *HHT.*" *Malay Literature* Vol. 25, No. 2 (2012): 229–60.

"*Hikayat Hang Tuah*: Malay Epic and Muslim Mirror: Some Considerations on Its Date, Meaning, and Structure." *Bijdragen tot de Taal-, Land- en Volkenkunde* 146.4 (1990): 399–412.

"Structure, date and sources of *Hikayat Aceh* revisited: The Problem of Mughal-Malay Literary Ties." *Bijdragen tot de Taal-, Land- en Volkenkunde* 162–64 (2006): 441–67.

The Turkic-Turkish Theme in Traditional Malay Literature: Imagining the Other to Empower the Self. Leiden: Brill, 2015.

Bronson, Bennet. "Exchange at the Upstream and Downstream Ends: Notes towards a Functional Model of the Coastal State in Southeast Asia." In *Economic Exchange and Social Interaction in Southeast Asia: Perspectives from Prehistory and Ethnography.* Ed. Karl L. Hutterer. Ann Arbor: Centre for South and Southeast Asian Studies, University Michigan, 1977, 39–52.

Brown, Piers. "'That full-sail voyage': Travel Narratives and Astronomical Discovery in Kepler and Galileo." In *The Invention of Discovery, 1500–1700.* Ed. James Dougal Fleming. Farnham and Burlington: Ashgate, 2011, 15–28.

Casale, Giancarlo. *The Ottoman Age of Exploration*. Oxford: Oxford University Press, 2010.

Catz, Rebecca. "Consequences and Repercussions of the Portuguese Expansion on Literature." *Portuguese Studies* Vol. 8 (1992): 115–23.

Certeau, Michel de. *The Practice of Everyday Life*. Trans. Steven F. Rendall, vol. 1. Berkeley and Los Angeles: University of California Press, 1984.

Chaudhuri, K. N. *Trade and Civilisation in the Indian Ocean: An Economic History from the Rise of Islam to 1750*. Cambridge: Cambridge University Press, 1985.

Cook, Harold J. *Matters of Exchange: Commerce, Medicine, and Science in the Dutch Golden Age*. New Haven, CT: Yale University Press, 2008.

Costa, Palmira Fontes da, ed. *Medicine, Trade and Empire: Garcia de Orta's* Colloquies on the Simples and Drugs of India *(1563) in Context*. London: Routledge, 2016. First pub. Ashgate, 2015.

Crawfurd, John. *A Descriptive Dictionary of the Indian Islands & Adjacent Countries*. London: Bradbury & Evans, 1856.

Daehnhardt, Rainer. *The Bewitched Gun: The Introduction of the Firearm in the Far East by the Portuguese*. Lisbon: Texto Editora, 1994.

Day, Tony, and Craig J. Reynolds. "Cosmologies, Truth Regimes, and the State in Southeast Asia." *Modern Asian Studies* Vol. 34, No. 1 (2000): 1–55.

Deshpande, Anirudh. "The Indian Fort As a Site of Intersections." In *Narratives, Routes and Intersections in Pre-modern Asia*. Ed. Radhika Seshan. London: Routledge, 2017, 126–45.

Drakard, Jane. *A Malay Frontier: Unity and Duality in a Sumatran Kingdom*. Ithaca, NY: Southeast Asia Program Publications, Cornell University, 1990.

Eamon, William. *Science and the Secrets of Nature: Books of Secrets in Medieval and Early Modern Culture*. Princeton, NJ: Princeton University Press, 2004.

Eaton, Richard M. "'Kiss my foot,' said the King: Firearms, Diplomacy and the Battle of Raichur, 1520." *Modern Asian Studies* Vol. 43, No. 1 (2009): 289–313.

Eco, Umberto. *Experiences in Translation*. Trans. Alastair McEwen. Toronto: University of Toronto Press, 2001.

Emmerson, Donald. "The Case for a Maritime Perspective on Southeast Asia." *Journal of Southeast Asian Studies* Vol. 11 (1980): 139–45.

Ferrand, Gabriel. "Malaka: le Malayu et Malayur." *Journal Asiatique* Vol. 11 (1918): 391–484; 12 (1918): 51–154.

Figueira, Dorothy. "Race in Classical Literature and Portuguese and Italian Travel Narratives." In *Travel Writing and Cultural Memory/Écriture du*

Voyage et Mémoire Culturelle. Vol. 9 of the Proceedings of the XVth Congress of the International Comparative Literature Association. Ed. Maria Alziro Seixo. Amsterdam: Rodopi, 2000, 253–64.

Fleming, James Dougal, ed. *The Invention of Discovery, 1500–1700*. Farnham: Ashgate, 2011.

Flint, Valerie I. J. *The Imaginative Landscape of Christopher Columbus*. Princeton, NJ: Princeton University Press, 1992.

Flores, Jorge. "Between Madrid and Ophir: Erédia, a Deceitful Discoverer?" In *Dissimulation and Deceit in Early Modern Europe*. Ed. Miriam Eliav-Feldon and Tamar Herzig. New York: Palgrave Macmillan, 2015, 184–210.

"Distant Wonders: The Strange and the Marvelous between Mughal India and Habsburg Iberia in the Early Seventeenth Century." *Comparative Studies in Society and History* Vol. 49, No. 3 (2007): 553–81.

"Two Portuguese Visions of Jahangir's India: Jerónimo Xavier and Manuel Godinho de Erédia." In *Goa and the Great Mughal*. Ed. Jorge Flores and Nuno Vassallo e Silva. Lisbon: Calouste Gulbenkian Foundation, 2004, 44–67.

Unwanted Neighbours: The Mughals, the Portuguese, and Their Frontier Zones. New Delhi: Oxford University Press, 2018.

Franklin-Brown, Mary. *Reading the World: Encyclopedic Writing in the Scholastic Age*. Chicago, IL: University of Chicago Press, 2012.

Fuchs, Barbara. *Romance*. New York: Routledge, 2004.

Geertz, Clifford. "Deep Play: Notes on the Balinese Cockfight." In *The Interpretation of Cultures: Selected Essays*. New York: Basic Books, 1973, 2000, 412–53.

Gibson-Hill, Carl Alexander "The Malay Annals: The History Brought from Goa." *Journal of the Malayan Branch of the Royal Asiatic Society* Vol. 29, No. 1 (1956): 185–88.

Godinho, Vitorino Magalhães. "A ideia de descobrimento e os descobrimentos e expansão." *Anais do Clube Militar Naval* Vol. CXX (Oct.–Dec. 1990): 627–42.

Greenblatt, Stephen. *Shakespearean Negotiations: The Circulation of Social Energy in Renaissance England*. Berkeley: University of California Press, 1988.

Gunn, Geoffrey C. *Imagined Geographies: The Maritime Silk Roads in World History, 100–1800*. Hong Kong: Hong Kong University Press, 2022.

Heesterman, Johannes Cornelis "Littoral et intérieur de l'Inde." *Itinerario* Vol. 4, No. 1 (1980): 87–92.

Hespanha, António Manuel. *Filhos da terra: Identidades mestiças nos confins da expansão Portuguesa*. Lisbon: Tinta-da-China, 2019.

Hooker, Virginia Matheson, and Anthony C. Milner. *Perceptions of the Hajj. Five Malay Texts*. Singapore: Institute of Southeast Asian Studies, 1984.

Hooykaas, Christiaan. *Over Maleise literatuur*. 2nd ed. Leiden: E. J. Brill, 1937.

Hosten, Henri, ed. and trans. "Description of Indostan and Guzarate by Manuel Godinho de Eredia (1611)." *Journal of the Royal Asiatic Society of Bengal* Vol. 4 (1938): 533–66.

Kathirithamby-Wells, Jeyamalar. "Hulu-Hilir Unity and Conflict: Malay Statecraft in East Sumatra before the Mid-Nineteenth Century." *Archipel* Vol. 45 (1993): 77–96.

Khan, Iqtidar Alam. "Early Use of Cannons and Musket in India." *Journal of Economic and Social History of the Orient* Vol. 24, No. 2 (1980): 158–63.

"Firearms in Central Asia and Iran During the Fifteenth Century and the Origins and Nature of Firearms Brought by Babur." *Proceedings of the Indian History Congress* Vol. 56 (1995): 435–46.

Gunpowder and Firearms: Warfare in Medieval India. New Delhi: Oxford University Press, 2004.

Khan, M. A. Muid. "Indo-Portuguese Struggle for Maritime Supremacy (as gleaned from an unpublished Arabic urjuza: Fathul Mubiyn)." In *Studies in the Foreign Relations of India (From Earliest Times to 1947): Prof. H. K. Sherwani Felicitation Volume*. Ed. P. M. Joshi and M. A. Nayeem. Hyderabad: State Archives, Government of Andhra Pradesh, 1975, 165–83.

Khanna, Neetu. *The Visceral Logics of Decolonization*. Durham, NC: Duke University Press, 2020.

Kooria, Mahmood. "'Killed the Pilgrims and Persecuted Them': Portuguese *Estado da India*'s Encounters with the Hajj in the Sixteenth Century." In *The Hajj and Europe in the Age of Empire*. Ed. Umar Ryad. Leiden: Brill, 2017, 14–46.

Lefevere, André. "Composing the Other." In *Post-colonial Translation: Theory and Practice*. Ed. Susan Bassnett and Harish Trivedi. London: Routledge, 2002, 75–94.

Loureiro, Rui Manuel. *A biblioteca de Diogo do Couto*. Macau: Instituto Cultural de Macau, 1998.

Macgregor, Ian A. "Johore Lama in the Sixteenth Century." *Journal of the Malayan Branch of the Royal Asiatic Society* Vol. 28, No. 2(1955): 48–126.

Maier, Henk M. J. "An Epik That Never Was an Epic: The Malay *Hikayat Hang Tuah*." In *Epic Adventures: Heroic Narrative in the Oral Performance Traditions of Four Continents*. Ed. Jan Jansen and Henk M. J. Maier. Münster: LIT, 2004, 112–27.

Major, Richard Henry. *The Discovery of Australia by the Portuguese in 1601, Five Years before the Earliest Discovery Hitherto Recorded*. London: J. B. Nichols and Sons, 1861.

"Further Facts in the History of the Early Discovery of Australia." *Archaeologia* Vol. 44, No. 2 (1874): 233–41.

Marsden, William. *The History of Sumatra*. London, 1811.

May, Sally K., Paul S. C. Taçon, Daryl Wesley, and Michael Pearson. "Painted Ships on a Painted Arnhem Land Landscape." *The Great Circle* Vol. 35, No. 2 (2013): 83–102.

Meilink-Roelofsz, Marie Antoinette Petronella. *Asian Trade and European Influence in the Indonesian Archipelago between 1500 and about 1650*. The Hague: Martinus Nijhoff, 1962.

Murad, Auda. *Merantau: Outmigration in a Matrilineal Society of West Sumatra*. Canberra: Australian National University, Department of Demography, 1980.

Nasution, Khoo Salma. *The Chulia in Penang: Patronage and Place-making around the Kapitan King Mosque, 1786–1957*. Penang: Areca Books, 2014.

Netton, Ian Richard. "Riḥla." *Encyclopaedia of Islam, Second Edition*. Ed. B. Lewis et al. Leiden: Brill 1995. Vol. 8, p. 32.

Ng, Su Fang. *Alexander the Great from Britain to Southeast Asia: Peripheral Empires in the Global Renaissance*. Oxford: Oxford University Press, 2019.

"Making Race in the Early Modern East Indies." *New Literary History* Vol. 52, No. 3/4 (2021): 509–33.

Ngai, Sianne. *Ugly Feelings*. Cambridge, MA: Harvard University Press, 2005.

Noorduyn, Jacobus. "Concerning the Reliability of Tomé Pires' Data on Java." *Bijdragen tot de Taal-, Land- en Volkenkunde* Vol. 132, No. 4 (1976): 467–71.

Padrón, Ricardo. "Hybrid Maps: Cartography and Literature in Spanish Imperial Expansion, Sixteenth Century." In *Literature and Cartography: Theories, Histories, Genres*. Ed. Anders Engberg-Peterson. Cambridge, MA: MIT Press, 2017, 199–217.

The Indies of the Setting Sun: How Early Modern Spain Mapped the Far East as the Transpacific West. Chicago, IL: University of Chicago Press, 2020.

The Spacious Word: Cartography, Literature, and Empire in Early Modern Spain. Chicago, IL: University of Chicago Press, 2004.

Parker, Geoffrey. *The Military Revolution: Military Innovation and the Rise of the West, 1500*–1800. 2nd ed. Cambridge: Cambridge University Press, 1996.

Parnickle, Boris Borisovitch. "An Epic Hero and an 'Epic Traitor' in the *Hikayat Hang Tuah*." *Bijdragen tot de Taal-, Land- en Volkenkunde* Vol. 132, No. 4 (1976): 403–17.

Pearson, Michael N. "Littoral Society: The Concept and the Problems." *Journal of World History* Vol. 17, No. 4 (2006): 353–73.

Pious Passengers: The Hajj in Earlier Times. New Delhi: Sterling, 1994.

The Portuguese in India. Cambridge: Cambridge University Press, 1987.

Pelliot, Paul. "Le Hōja et le Sayyid Ḥusain de l'Histoire des Ming." *T'oung Pao*, second series, Vol. 38, No. 2/5 (1948): 81–292.

Phillips, Kim M. "Travel, Writing, and the Global Middle Ages." *History Compass* Vol. 14, No. 3 (2016): 81–92.

Pinto, Paulo Jorge de Sousa. *The Portuguese and the Straits of Melaka: 1575–1619: Power, Trade and Diplomacy*. Singapore: National University of Singapore Press, 2012.

Reid, Anthony. "Introduction: Slavery and Bondage in Southeast Asian History." In *Slavery, Bondage and Dependency in Southeast Asia*. Ed. Anthony Reid. St. Lucia: University of Queensland Press, 1983, 1–43.

"Sixteenth-century Turkish Influence in Western Indonesia." *Journal of South-East Asian History* Vol. 10, No. 3 (1969): 395–414.

Ricci, Ronit. *Islam Translated: Literature, Conversion, and the Arabic Cosmopolis of South and Southeast Asia*. Chicago, IL: University of Chicago Press, 2011.

Roff, William R. "Islamic Institutions in Muslim Southeast Asia and Cognate Phenomena in the Indian Sub-continent." In *Islam in Southern Asia: a Survey of Current Research*. Ed. Dietmar Rothermund. Wiesbaden: Franz Steiner, 1975, 10–12.

"Pilgrimage and the History of Religions: Theoretical Approaches to the *Hajj*." In *Approaches to Islam in Religious Studies*. Ed. Richard C. Martin. Tucson: University of Arizona Press, 1985, 78–86.

Rosa, Fernando. *The Portuguese in the Creole Indian Ocean: Essays in Historical Cosmopolitanism*. Basingstoke: Palgrave Macmillan, 2015.

Rouffaer, Gerrit Pieter. "Was Malaka Emporium vóór 1400 A.D. genaamd Malajoer? En waar lag Woerawari, Ma-Hasin, Langka, Batoesawar?" *Bijdragen tot de Taal-, Land- en Volkenkunde* Vol. 77 (1921): 1–174, 359–604.

Rubiés, Joan-Pau. *Travel and Ethnology in the Renaissance: South India through European Eyes, 1250–1625*. Cambridge: Cambridge University Press, 2000.

"Travel Writing and Ethnography." In *The Cambridge Companion to Travel Writing*. Ed. Peter Hulme and Tim Youngs. Cambridge: Cambridge University Press, 2002, 242–60.

"Travel Writing As a Genre: Facts, Fictions and the Invention of a Scientific Discourse in Early Modern Europe." *Journeys* Vol. 1 (2000): 5–35.

Russell-Wood, Anthony John R. *The Portuguese Empire, 1415–1808: A World on the Move*. Baltimore, MD: Johns Hopkins University Press, 1998.

Sell, Jonathan. *Rhetoric and Wonder in English Travel Writing, 1560–1613*. Aldershot: Ashgate, 2006.

Sen, Amrita. "Solomon, Ophir, and the English Quest for the East Indies." In *England's Asian Renaissance*. Ed. Su Fang Ng and Carmen Nocentelli. Newark: University of Delaware Press, 2022, 125–42.

Serjeant, Robert B. *The Portuguese off the South Arabian Coast: Hadhrami Chronicles with Yemeni and European Accounts of Dutch Pirates off Mocha in the Seventeenth Century*. Oxford: Clarendon Press, 1963.

Sewell, Robert. *A Forgotten Empire (Vijayanagar): A Contribution to the History of India*. London: Swan Sonnenschein, 1900.

Sheehan, Kevin. "Science and Patronage in the Pacific Voyage of Pedro Fernández de Quirós, 1605–1606." In *Science in the Spanish and Portuguese Empires, 1500–1800*. Ed. Daniela Bleichmar, Paula de Vos, Kristin Huffine, and Kevin Sheehan. Stanford, CA: Stanford University Press, 2008, 233–46.

Skinner, Cyril. "Transitional Malay Literature: Part 1 Ahmad Rijaluddin and Munshi Abdullah." *Bijdragen tot de Taal-, Land- en Volkenkunde* Vol. 134, No. 4 (1978): 466–87.

Smith, Estellie M. *Those Who Live from the Sea: A Study in Maritime Anthropology*. Saint Paul, MN: West, 1977.

Subrahmanyan, Sanjay. "Between a Rock and Hard Place: Some Afterthoughts." In *The Brokered World: Go-Betweens and Global Intelligence, 1770–1820*. Ed. Simon Schaffer, Lissa Roberts, Raj Kapil, and James Delbourgo. Sagamore Beach, MA: Watson Publishing International, 2009, 429–40.

Courtly Encounters: Translating Courtliness and Violence in Early Modern Eurasia. Cambridge, MA: Harvard University Press, 2012.

The Political Economy of Commerce: Southern India 1500–1650. Cambridge: Cambridge University Press, 2002.

The Portuguese Empire in Asia, 1500–1700: A Political and Economic History. 2nd ed. Chichester: Wiley-Blackwell, 2012.

"What the Tamils Said: A Letter from the Kelings of Melaka (1527)." *Archipel* Vol. 82 (2011): 137–58.

Subrahmanyam, Sanjay, and Geoffrey Parker. "Arms and the Asian: Revisiting European Firearms and Their Place in Early Modern Asia." *Armas, Fortalezas e Revista de Cultura* Vol. 26 (2008): 12–42.

Swettenham, Frank Athelstane. *British Malaya: An Account of the Origin and Progress of British Influence in Malaya*. Rev. ed. London: George Allen and Unwin, 1948.

Taçon, Paul S. C., Sally K. May, Stewart J. Fallon, Meg Travers, Daryl Wesley, and Ronald Lamilami. "A Minimum Age for Early Depictions of Southeast Asian Praus in the Rock Art of Arnhem Land, Northern Territory." *Australian Archaeology* Vol. 71, No. 1 (2010): 1–10.

Tagliacozzo, Eric. *The Longest Journey: Southeast Asians and the Pilgrimage to Mecca*. New York: Oxford University Press, 2013.

Tambiah, Stanley J. "The Galactic Polity: The Structure of Political Kingdoms in Southeast Asia." *Annals of the New York Academy of Sciences* Vol. 293, No. 1 (1977): 69–97.

Thomaz, Luís Filipe F. R. "Estrutura Politica e Administrativa do Estado da Índia no Século XVI." In Luís Filipe F. R. Thomaz, *De Ceuta a Timor*. Lisbon: Difel, 1994, 207–43. First published in *Actas do II Seminário Internacional de História Indo-Portuguesa*. Ed. Luís de Albuquerque and Inácio Guerreiro. Lisbon: Instituto de Investigação Científica Tropical Centro de Estudos de História e Cartografia Antiga, 1985, 513–40.

"L'idee imperiale Manueline." In *La decouverte, le Portugal et l'Europe, Acts du Colloque Paris, les 26, 27 et 28 mai 1988*. Ed. Jean Aubin. Paris: Fondation Calouste Gulbenkian, 1990.

"Malaka et ses communautés marchandes au tournant du 16e siècle." In *Marchands et hommes d'affaires asiatiques dans l'Océan Indien et la Mer de Chine 13e-20e siècles*. Ed. Denys Lombard and Jean Aubin. Paris: Éditions de l'École des Hautes Études en Sciences Sociales, 1988, 31–48.

Touati, H. *Islam and Travel in the Middle Ages*. Trans. L. G. Cochrane. Chicago, IL: University of Chicago Press, 2010.

Turnbull, Stephen. *The Lost Samurai: Japanese Mercenaries in South East Asia*, 1593–1688. Barnsley, PA: Frontline Books, 2021.

Villamar, Cuauhtémoc. *Portuguese Merchants in the Manila Galleon System: 1565–1600*. New York: Routledge, 2020.

Wade. Geoff. "The Zheng He Voyages: A Reassessment." *Journal of the Malaysian Branch of the Royal Asiatic Society* Vol. 78.1, No. 288 (2005): 37–58.

Wake, Christopher. "Banten around the Turn of the Sixteenth Century: Trade and Society in an Indonesian Port City." In *Gateways to Asia: Port Cities of Asia in the 13th–20th Centuries*. Ed. Frank Broeze. London: Paul Keegan, 1997, 66–108.

"Malacca's Early Kings and the Reception of Islam." *Journal of Southeast Asian History* Vol. 5, No. 2 (1964): 104–28.

Walker, Andrew. *The Legend of the Golden Boat: Regulation, Trade and Traders in the Borderlands of Laos, Thailand, China and Burma*. Richmond, Surrey: Curzon Press, 1999.

Wang, Gungwu. "China and Southeast Asia, 1402–1424." In *Studies in the Social History of China and Southeast Asia: Essays in Memory of Victor Purcell*. Ed. Jerome Ch'en and Nicholas Tarling. Cambridge: Cambridge University Press, 1970, 375–402.

"The Opening of Relations between China and Malacca, 1403–05." In *Malayan and Indonesian Studies: Essays Presented to Sir Richard Winstedt on His 85th Birthday*. Ed. John S. Bastin and Roelof Roolvink. London: Oxford University Press, 1964, 87–104.

Whitehead, Neil. "South America/Amazonia: The Forest of Marvels." In *The Cambridge Companion to Travel Writing*. Ed. Peter Hulme and Tim Youngs. Cambridge: Cambridge University Press, 2002, 122–38.

Wink, André. *Al-Hind: Early Medieval India and the Expansion of Islam, 7th–11th Centuries*. Leiden: Brill, 2002.

Xavier, Ângela Barreto, and Ines G. Županov. *Catholic Orientalism: Portuguese Empire, Indian Knowledge (16th–18th Centuries)*. New Delhi: Oxford University Press, 2015.

Yule, Henry, Sir. *Hobson-Jobson: A Glossary of Colloquial Anglo-Indian Words and Phrases, and of Kindred Terms, Etymological, Historical, Geographical and Discursive*. New ed. William Crooke. London: J. Murray, 1903.

Acknowledgments

This project was in many ways a journey home, as Melaka was my late father's hometown. It is the culmination of thinking that has been profoundly shaped and helped by many scholars and institutions over the years, for which I am grateful, though I mention only a few here. I would specifically like to thank the series editors, Tim Youngs and, especially, Nandini Das, for their encouragement, and the Editorial Assistant Edgar Mendez for his help and patience. Two anonymous readers made this work far better. A Niles grant from Virginia Tech's College of Liberal Arts and Human Sciences gave me the much-needed time to complete the manuscript. I am indebted to Josiah Blackmore, from whose work I learnt much, for securing an article I was unable to obtain through interlibrary loan. Finally, I thank Kenneth Hodges for his support during these challenging times. I dedicate this Element to my parents; I wish my father could have lived to see its publication.

Travel Writing

Nandini Das

University of Oxford

Nandini Das is a literary scholar and cultural historian, Professor of Early Modern Literature and Culture at the University of Oxford, and Fellow of Exeter College, Oxford. With Tim Youngs, she has co-edited *The Cambridge History of Travel Writing* (2019) and published widely on early modern English literature, cross-cultural encounters, and travel accounts.

Tim Youngs

Nottingham Trent University

Tim Youngs is Professor of English and Travel Studies at Nottingham Trent University. His books include *The Cambridge Companion to Travel Writing* (edited with Peter Hulme, 2002), *The Cambridge Introduction to Travel Writing* (2013), and *The Cambridge History of Travel Writing* (edited with Nandini Das, 2019). He edits the journal *Studies in Travel Writing*.

About the Series

Travel writing is enormously varied. It consists of several different forms and has a long history across many cultures. This series aims to reflect that diversity, offering exciting studies of a range of travel texts and topics. The Elements further advance the latest thinking in travel writing, extending previous work and opening up the field to fresh readings and subjects of inquiry.

Cambridge Elements

Travel Writing

Elements in the Series

Eco-Travel: Journeying in the Age of the Anthropocene
Michael Cronin

Writing Tudor Exploration: Richard Eden and West Africa
Matthew Dimmock

Writing about Discovery in the Early Modern East Indies
Su Fang Ng

A full series listing is available at: www.cambridge.org/ELTW

Printed in the United States
by Baker & Taylor Publisher Services